MW00426506

THE WHOLE SHOT

THE WHOLE SHOT

COLLECTED INTERVIEWS WITH

GREGORY CORSO

EDITED WITH NOTES BY RICK SCHOBER
FOREWORD BY DICK BRUKENFELD

TOUGH POETS PRESS / ARLINGTON, MASSACHUSETTS

The Whole Shot: Collected Interviews with Gregory Corso

First Printing

ISBN 978-0-692-42713-2

Tough Poets Press
49 Churchill Avenue, Floor 2
Arlington, Massachusetts 02476
U.S.A.

www.toughpoets.com

For my wife and four daughters who sometimes pretended to listen whenever I mentioned Corso or this book project.

CONTENTS

FOREWORD
Dick Brukenfeld

We adopted Gregory Corso our senior year at Harvard. Three of my fellow students kept him in their Eliot House rooms for the 1954–55 school year. They hung a tie-dyed sheet across a corner of their living room to give Gregory a place to sleep. They brought back bowls of food from the dining hall to sustain him.

My contribution to the care and feeding of Corso was to publish his first collection of poetry, *The Vestal Lady on Brattle*. One afternoon as we strolled along the banks of the Charles River, Gregory announced he had enough poems to make a book but couldn't find a publisher. Although I knew little about poetry and less about publishing, I liked the vividness and eccentricity of Gregory's work. So with the confidence of untested youth, I volunteered to do the job.

Neither his poetry nor our fascination with Gregory came out of a vacuum. It's difficult today to imagine the 1950s – the up-tightness, the conformity, the repressed insanity that kept leaking out at the seams, and the nastiness those in power got away with. All of it was thriving at Harvard.

One nutty professor walked around the campus wielding his cane like a broadsword. He used it to poke, prod, and push students out of his way. Professor of Religion Arthur Darby Nock refused to share a path or sidewalk with students. Regarding them as cattle strayed from their pen, he would literally shove them aside – with impunity. Another professor whose bad deeds went unpunished was in Fine Arts, my major. An excellent teacher, the man had one serious flaw. A female student would be in his office discussing her work, when the next thing she knew, the professor was pinning her against the wall, panting like a dog in heat.

Then there was Harvard's way of delaying diversity by ghettoizing Jewish freshmen, placing them only with Jewish roommates. Not to mention that in our class of 1,000 plus, we had five African-American students. Still, we were not ones to complain out loud. We felt we were lucky to be there. The spirit of the age told us that father knew best – whether he be Harvard, a corporation, or the government. As a graduate student warned, when I said I wanted to be a freelance writer, "No one is free. You either become part of an institution, or you belong in one."

Happily, Harvard and its Cambridge surroundings housed a group of artists and writers who yearned for a better, free spirited world. A bright star in this firmament, Violet "Bunny" Lang, brought Gregory Corso to Cambridge. Poet, playwright, actress, and co-founder of the Poets Theater, Bunny Lang was a passionate promoter of the arts and of people she believed in. She met Gregory at Allen Ginsberg's apartment in New York. Impressed with his charm and promise as a poet, she installed him in a room at 12 Ash St. Place which cost her $5 a week. Here the broke, homeless Corso would have a place to live and develop his work.

Gregory's next lucky break came as a blessing in disguise. The City of Cambridge told the owner of 12 Ash St. Place his house was not set up for renting rooms. Gregory would have to go. At this point Bunny Lang was feeling the effects of the Hodgkins disease that would kill her the following year at 32. Bunny asked the budding novelist Peter Sourian if he could help relocate Corso.

Sourian, a senior at Harvard, came up with the ingenious idea of keeping Gregory as a stowaway in Eliot House. Sourian and his roommates, Paul Grand and Bobby Sedgwick, did more than house and feed the poet. They brought him into the world of the university, sneaking him into lectures and other events. They introduced him to a wide network of friends, which opened the door for me to raise the money for publishing his *The Vestal Lady on Brattle*.

Gregory was a refreshing antidote to the rigidity of our world. We had come to Harvard via the conventional path of prep and high school. Gregory was a graduate of the streets of New York's Little Italy and Dannemora Prison, where he'd spent three years in the library educating himself. We loved his street-smart brashness, which was tempered by a survivor's wit and warmth.

Although he could erupt like Mt. Vesuvius, his angry blasts were brief and often created for theatrical effect. At a party in Eliot House, Gregory started yelling at a giant named Gene Higgins who could have picked him up with one hand. Corso made as if to throw his drink at Higgins. At the last moment, he threw his glass against the wall near but not at Higgins who, with a knowing look, stayed calm. Tantrum finished, Gregory chilled and resumed talking to the giant.

Corso loved Walt Whitman's poetry, its openness of subject matter and freedom of form. Like his Beat poet brothers, he objected to imposing rhyme and meter on his words. He believed the impulse for a poem would find its own organic form. In "This is America" from *The Vestal Lady on Brattle*, Gregory plays the hipster Walt Whitman. It begins:

> This is America and I'm fun in it
> with a wealth of music and lunatics
> with a mouth that cannot sing
> and I love a woman
> and hate the rest and I'll make it
> with anything female ten to fifty
> and fifty's best

He sounds a less rollicking note in "12 Ash St. Place," also from *The Vestal Lady on Brattle*. This isn't a song of praise to his first Cambridge sanctuary. Instead, he sees the house as sad, with an old man inside who drips colors from his hands. The old man drips purple onto Gregory's hand, and it burns. To me, Gregory is wrestling with his feelings about taking handouts, which is how he survived. He had a disarming way of asking for support, especially from women. Yet he's saying that taking handouts also burned his sense of self.

Most emphatically, publishing *The Vestal Lady on Brattle* was not a handout. It cost Gregory 10 months' labor to write and winnow the 36 included poems for which he received no money beyond one symbolic dollar. None of us were paid – not me for publishing the book, not Nick Cikovsky for designing the cover, nor Harvard teaching fellow David Wheeler who wrote the introduction under the pseudonym "P.L.B." All money went to the printer who delivered our edition of 300 copies in mid-May. Sales were less than brisk, as Corso's hosts and many friends graduated and left Cambridge a few weeks later. Yet as Gregory left for California, he took with him a valuable asset – a collection of his year's best work published by people who believed he deserved a wider audience.

After a brief detour in Los Angeles, Corso joined Allen Ginsberg and other Beat poet colleagues in San Francisco. It became their launching pad. Corso, Ginsberg, Philip Lamantia, Lawrence Ferlinghetti, and others took part in a series of poetry readings which were welcomed by large, enthusiastic audiences. Ferlinghetti's City Lights Bookstore photocopied *The*

Vestal Lady on Brattle I had published, and put out more books in a facsimile edition. As they became better known, Gregory and the other Beats helped to inspire the tidal wave of iconoclasm and revolt that marked the 1960s. Ginsberg and Corso rode that wave to increasing public recognition.

The interviews Rick Schober has collected for this book are part of that heady ride. Beginning with the bemused, sarcastic questioning of the humorist Art Buchwald, these interviews range to serious dialogues where Gregory opens up about his ways and means as a poet. Corso comes across as the entertaining, merry soul he was – and much more. Like all important artists, he tried to see things in his subjects no one had seen before.

At a moment when our culture is paying attention to the 1960s, these interviews give an insider's view of what was happening.

EDITOR'S INTRODUCTION

In researching material for this book, I came across a few interviews and recorded discussions with Gregory Corso that, ultimately, I chose not to include. My decision to remove these pieces from consideration was in no way a reflection on their quality. They were excluded solely because they did not meet the criteria I established when I started this project – namely, that Corso had to be the main voice and not a peripheral participant in the interview, and that the interview had to include some discussion of his poetry, literature in general, and/or the influence of the Beat writers on popular culture and society.

The most notable pieces omitted were "Discussion Following Poetry Reading, April 1973," which appeared in *Gone Soft*, Vol. 1, No. 3 (Salem State College, 1974); Corso's KCBO radio interview, which can be found in *Wings, Wands, Windows* (Englewood, CO: Howling Dog Press, 1982); J.G. Gosciak's "Tales of Beatnik Lore: An Interview with Gregory Corso" from *Contact II: A Poetry Review* (New York, Summer/Fall 1989); and "Gregory and His Daughter" from *Goodie Magazine*, No. 9 (New York, 2001).

The interviews that made the final cut for this collection have been reprinted in their entireties as originally published. The one exception is Corso's interview from the documentary *What Happened to Kerouac?* which has not appeared in print before. It was transcribed specifically for this book with the filmmaker's permission. The introductions to the interviews by Michael Andre and Gavin Selerie have been slightly abridged in accordance with their requests.

The years that appear above the titles indicate when the interviews took place, and not necessarily when they were first published. Edits have been limited to correcting obvious misspellings and standardizing punctuation, date formats, titles, etc. British spelling has been preserved in the two interviews that were originally published in the UK. Poems and poem fragments that appear in the interviews have been edited to reflect the punctuation, capitalization, and formatting of the original poems as published by City Lights Books and New Directions.

In a few places within the text, notes have been added inside of square brackets, either by me or by the interviews' original editors, to provide clarification (e.g., last names, page numbers, etc.). Whenever I came across a reference in the text that I was not familiar with and, if I felt that additional information regarding that reference might enhance someone else's reading experience, then I added a note. (Endnotes begin on page 187.) Finally, Corso and his interviewers dropped a lot of names during their conversations, some of which may not be familiar to the casual reader. Therefore, an appendix has been added to provide brief biographical information for the many literary figures mentioned throughout these interviews.

Rick Schober

" – but no more interviews."
Gregory Corso

From a June 1958 letter to writer LeRoi Jones [Amiri Baraka] shortly after Corso and Allen Ginsberg were interviewed by newspaper columnist Art Buchwald for his *New York Herald Tribune* article "Two Poets in Paris." Corso referred to the interview as "real nowhere and jerky" and later wrote that it "really got me wrong and showed me as a talkative idiot."

(Source: Bill Morgan, ed., *An Accidental Autobiography: The Selected Letters of Gregory Corso* (New York: New Directions, 2003), pp. 108–109.)

GREGORY SENDS US POEMS THAT WE DON'T GET
Murray Robinson

Two matters of poetry bobbed up recently on the same day. One was the arrival from Cambridge, Mass., of Gregory the Poet's first book of collected works. The other was the exit from New York of Lord Dunsany, the Irish poet-dramatist.

You may remember Gregory. New York slum kid turned poet. After discovering him last year writing horror poems in a secret tunnel, I've been keeping a pleased eye on his progress.

It is evidenced by his being taken up by a set of bewitched Harvards and the publication of his book, entitled *The Vestal Lady on Brattle and Other Poems*. The 1955 Gregory wears shoes instead of sneakers and uses his last name, which is Corso.

Now, it isn't to be inferred that Lord Dunsany headed for the high seas because Gregory's poems came to town. But before sailing, he did utter certain crisp remarks about new-type poets which catty critics might say applied to Gregory and his works.

"When you see nonsense," Lord Dunsany cracked, "say it's nonsense. Don't say to yourself, 'I, poor lowbrow, am not clever enough to understand it.' Too often, modern verse is nothing but long, rambling, unintelligible prose."

A few days later Gregory telephoned. "Did you get my book?" he asked.

"I got the book," he was told, "but I don't get the poems." Then I quoted Lord Dunsany to him, assuring him that there was nothing personal intended.

He snorted long distance. "Never heard of any Dunsany," he said grandly. "Yeats, yes. Dunsany, no. And suppose you can't understand some of my poems. Like Archibald MacLeish said, 'A poem should not mean, but be.'"

Some of Gregory's works fill that order. They may not mean, but they sure are. Thirty-seven [36] poems in all in his book. Some first appeared here [*New York World-Telegram & Sun*], and in the *Cambridge Review*, the *Harvard Advocate*, and *The Pelican* at the University of California. Most of the collection, I'm sure, will be huzzahed by the type [of] people who say they understand progressive jazz and abstract painting.

In "The Vestal Lady on Brattle," Gregory sings that the old dame on that famed street pours "old milk for an old cat." I figured he booted one here. Even an old dame on Brattle would have more sense than to pour old milk for an old cat, because even an old cat wouldn't drink old milk.

"Damn all realism," Gregory cried bitterly. "I write from the soul. It would shrivel if I wrote she poured *fresh* milk for an old cat."

He added: "Did you ever meet a poet you could understand? I did. It's boring."

Gregory isn't boring by the yardstick, like when he wrote "The Sausages." It goes:

> I ate sausages with you at the feast.
> I ate sausages, and across the street
> the butcher counted his daughter's feet!

(Couldn't have taken the butcher long, unless she were a centipede, and judging from Gregory's whimsical turn of mind, I'd say she was.)

Equally baffling is "Into the Aperture of an Unlikely Archimage" which begins:

> On coming past a thing of hand
> autochthonic like dirt my hand ...

But then some of Gregory's poems seem to mean as well as be, although *I* can't quite figure out what they mean. For instance, "Song":

> Oh, dear! Oh, me! Oh, my!
> I married the pig's daughter!
> Why? Why? Why?

He answers this three-ply question in the last stanza:

Because I felt I had oughta!

Yes, indeed, Gregory is going places with the opaque poetry set. But that's not all. While at Cambridge, he wrote a one-act play which stood up under three performances there. It's title, *In This Hung-Up Age*.

"Even *you* can get that," Gregory said. "It's all about a buffalo killing people."

TWO POETS IN PARIS
Art Buchwald

PARIS

The so-called "beat generation" of the United States hasn't made too much of a mark on Paris. But thanks to two American poets, Allen Ginsberg and Gregory Corso, things are looking up. Mr. Ginsberg, who went to Columbia University, and Mr. Corso, who came out of Dannemora Prison, have been traveling around Europe reading their poems and preaching the gospel of the new American poetry.

"We've changed the course of poetry in the United States," said Mr. Ginsberg. "Do you realize what that means? There's been a revolution in poetry and we've done it. There's no equivalent to it in France. England is dead. They're in the cellar with iambic."

"Dame Edith Sitwell," said Mr. Corso, "told us the hope of English poetry is in America. She also gave us tea and watercress sandwiches."

Mr. Ginsberg tried to explain exactly what the beat generation had done for poetry. "We're experimenting, we have a new basis of measure. We measure our lines by breath, not by beat. Give us time and we'll take over from the priests. We have a message. People have to understand. Our mission is to make them."

"The square poets," said Mr. Corso, "don't dig what we're doing. Their horror is they take their form from Auden's first page 'In Breughel's Icarus for instance ...' and Marianne Moore's 'Dürer would have liked living in this town.' None of their poems start with 'Fried shoes.' Our poetry is Wham-bam. Whatever comes to our mind. That's our message."

Mr. Corso, who has a book of poems called *Gasoline*, is 28 years old. He spent three years in Dannemora for robbery and got out when he was 20 years old. Unlike many men who leave prison, Mr. Corso said he found love and beauty in prison and the books he read there made him decide to be a poet.

As a poet he said he's taken a vow of poverty, but he added: "It's hard to live up to it because I like Lucifer too much."

"How do you get by?" we asked.

"It isn't easy," said Mr. Corso. "None of the foundations will give us any money. They don't dig us. I get money from girls. Every time I meet a girl I ask her how much money she has and then I demand half of it. I'm not doing anything wrong with the money. I just use it to buy food."

Things haven't been too easy for the two poets even when they have an opportunity to read their poetry. In Paris two months ago they held a reading in the Mistral, a Left Bank book shop. There were 40 or 50 people in attendance.

"Unfortunately," said Mr. Ginsberg, "another poet was reciting some uncommunicative junk and we didn't like it."

"I protested it wasn't real poetry," Mr. Corso said. "Someone asked me what I meant by real poetry. So I took off all my clothes and read my poems naked."

"Did they get the message?"

"I had two big bearded friends of mine as bodyguards and they threatened they'd beat up anybody who left while I was reciting. It was a big success."

"It was a mild reading," said Mr. Ginsberg, "compared so some I've been to in San Francisco."

Both poets were invited to read at Oxford to a group of about 100 students. For the occasion, Mr. Corso wrote a poem in praise of the atom bomb.

Oxford students have been protesting against the atom and hydrogen bombs and Mr. Corso's poem didn't go over too well.

Part of it went:

> BOOM all ye skies and BOOM all ye suns BOOM ye moons
> and ye stars BOOM and ye nights BOOM;
> BOOM ye days and BOOM ye winds, ye clouds,
>   ye rains, BOOM BOOM
> BANGBOOM ye lakes BING-Bangboom ye rivers bing

> BANGBBOOM ye forests;
> Yes! Yes! When the first bomb died
> flowers leapt in joy their roots aching;
> Fields knelt proud beneath the halleluyahs of the wind!
> Pink bombs blossomed! Elkbombs perked their ears;
> Ah many a bomb that day did awe the bird a gentle look –[1]

At about this point someone in the audience threw a shoe at Mr. Corso.

"It wasn't even a good English shoe," Mr. Corso complained. "Some idiot asked me after I read the poem how would I like to die by a bomb. He missed the whole point. What I was saying is that you should rise above the bomb. You shouldn't hate it, you should love it. Intelligent people are the only ones who can love. If people love they won't destroy. They didn't dig it. We called them all creeps and left. Only the girls followed us out to talk to us."

Even Pablo Picasso didn't dig Mr. Corso. Mr. Corso met the master in the south of France. "I've got a thing about brown. Brown to me is biscuits which taste like sardines to the tongue of God. I asked Picasso what he thought of brown and he thought I was talking about the color. When I told him what I really meant he hit me over the head with his hat. He shouldn't have hit me."

"What did you tell him?"

"I said: 'All love to poetry and nuts to painters.'"

The poets have voracious appetites. When Mr. Ginsberg met Marcel Duchamp, the French painter, he said: "I ate his shoe."

"Why?"

"To show him I hated even his shoe."

At the same party Mr. Corso was talking with Man Ray, the photographer and painter.

"Man Ray was eating a green cookie," said Mr. Corso, "and I asked him why he didn't eat the white ones. He said he only ate things the color of his tie. So I ate his tie."

"Why?"

"To show him I dug him. But I got sick."

Both poets feel they've given all they can to Paris. Mr. Ginsberg wants to go back to America if he can raise the fare, and Mr. Corso wants to go to India.

Paris won't be the same without them.

THE UPBEAT BEATNIK
Art Buchwald

PARIS

The last time we saw our good friend the beat poet Gregory Corso, he was struggling to be heard in a world filled with squares. But in less than a year and a half the picture, according to him, has changed and beatniks are here to stay.

Mr. Corso, who recently returned from a successful tour of American universities where they let him read his poetry, told us: "Beatniks in America are now a majority, even though they're still being treated like a minority. Every face you see is a beatnik face. It won't be long before everyone will sit in bed and eat big fat pies."

The philosophy of the beatniks, Mr. Corso explained to us, was that no man should work. "They got machines now to do the work," he said. "People got to start thinking. That's what's going to save us. Everyone staying in bed eating big fat pies and thinking. As soon as the bankers become beatniks they'll open the vaults and then everyone will have money."

We asked Mr. Corso how he explained the success of the beatniks in such a short time.

"We owe it all to Henry Luce."[1]

"How's that?"

"Well, when we first started, the literary magazines tried to put us down. But they had no luck, so they asked Henry Luce to help them. They said: 'Henry, we ain't got the circulation to stop them. It's up to you.' So Mr. Luce put *Time*, *Life*, *Fortune*, and *Sports Illustrated* at their disposal.

"Well, the elevators in the Time and Life Building went on a twenty-four-hour shift and everyone went to work. Pretty soon they were writing all about us. But instead of it becoming a drag, they were spreading the gospel faster than Western Union. People that never heard of beatniks suddenly became aware of us, and the little Frankenstein zoomed.

"Pretty soon it got just too much for Luce. One of his boys was sent out to interview us and he never went back. He gave up his worldly goods and he's now sitting underneath the Acropolis muttering about centaurs and Minotaurs.

"When Luce saw there was nothing he could do, he called in J. Edgar Hoover and the cops and said: 'This thing is bigger than me and Mrs. Luce.'

"So J. Edgar Hoover called the cops out and they started raiding coffee houses. They were even thinking of having a Sullivan law[2] for poets. They wanted to make it a criminal offense to carry a poem on your person. I had an arsenal at home – maybe 150 poems.

"But the cops got nowhere because instead of making arrests they started writing poetry to each other. Where can a thing like this end? The beatniks are a plague and the plague is on."

Mr. Corso said that during his travels in the United States he found a great interest in poetry. "People are getting hooked on poetry," he said. "It's like dope. Whether the beatniks did it with notoriety or silliness, America is getting conscious of poetry. When they start locking poets up, man, you know we've arrived.

"I even have college kids now who write to me and ask me how to become beatniks."

"What do you reply?"

"I say: 'I'm no Norman Vincent Peale.[3] You got to find it in your own way.' A lot of them are laying their arsenal of poems on me and they want me to comment on them. But I can't comment on poetry. When a man sings out something, it's marvelous just to have the song.

"This is going to be a great age," he said. "I can feel it. If we can only get some beatniks in the armies of the world, we can burn down war."

"How?" we wanted to know.

"All you have to do is get beatniks into an army and they'll do away with the uniforms. Now an army can't fight without uniforms. It's no fun. So instead, everybody will stay in their barracks and write poetry. Of course, the colonels will write better poetry than the captains, the captains will write better poetry than the sergeants, and the privates will get all the rejection slips."

So far, though, Mr. Corso said, beatniks haven't become rich. "The concept of an artist starving to death to paint good is going out. Maybe next it will be the poets. There would be nothing more perfect or beautiful than an elegant beatnik. We would bring back redlined capes, velvet suits, and big bow ties."

"What about baths?"

"We're not against baths. Henry Luce thinks we're against baths. In order for him to distinguish, he has to say there are people who smell nice and there are people who don't."

"Have you ever met Mr. Luce?" we asked him.

"You don't have to meet him," Mr. Corso said. "He's everywhere."

FROM AN INTERVIEW:
ON THE "BEAT MOVEMENT"

Anselm Hollo

Editor's note: As the title suggests, the following piece is an excerpt from a longer interview. However, all attempts to find a copy of the full transcription of the dialogue between poets Anselm Hollo and Gregory Corso, or even any record of its existence, were unsuccessful. In the credits of the Autumn 1962 issue of Nomad, *the magazine in which this originally appeared, the editors wrote "For permission ... we are indebted to Charge Records and Anselm Hollo for the interview by Gregory Corso." There was a small label named Charge Records releasing rhythm and blues 45s in New York City during the early 1960s but it is uncertain if this is the same one referred to in the magazine.*

HOLLO: Now, "Beat Movement" means what – that the movement that, let's say, we gave a thrust to, was to be a movement of poets getting up reading their poetry? Is that what you mean?

CORSO: Oh well, that would be absurd – to get up and say, well here this is what I'm doing and now I hope everybody else does this – No. I believe that you have to have something to fall back on, you have to have it, and it should always be You – it should never Follow, from something else – that's where the danger of Fad and Monotony can get into it by the Relay...

Now, "Beat Movement," if there was anything intended by that – to take the other angle – if it was something as a movement then it was for people to Wake Up! The poetry that was read by myself and Allen and a few others at the time was not altogether social, but a lot of it was Social – and a lot of it has come true: what we said – and a change in the Consciousness has happened.

Now a beat person in the United States is not a person who has a beard – exactly. The consciousness is changed by the beat – it is entering the lives of people who go to college, who are married, who have children. They do not, then, by their learning lock themselves up in a room and sleep on floors and don't take baths: that's not It – the Consciousness has altered there through everyone ... it has changed completely now and taste has become refined.

What once took a hundred years seems to take a decade now; one doesn't read what was said but one listens to what is being said – I think the main thing of the readings and the poems and all of it that came out was meant to aid and benefit man – to blend with the new consciousness! It was to give sounding that Here it is and to get everything into that light, see it into that light. So therefore I think that the Beat really have done something tremendous and beautiful. And I'm only down on the fact that the beat today – who came up as beat – are being Monsters of Frankenstein Replicas of the Mass Media – of the newspaper interpretation of Beat. But as for, let's say the original standards of the Beat – and it's almost I think as important as the Early Prophets – what the Beat did was to speak of Love, and it was to benefit man, and nothing else.

It was Me – but in association with Everyone: the lyric poem itself is "I," but it associates with all Man, and therefore it is a compassionate form of Poesie. A poet is supposed to See: and what he Sees, he puts within himself – and records outwardly – in Poetry.

1964

SOME OF MY BEGINNING ...
AND WHAT I FEEL RIGHT NOW
Gregory Corso

Editor's note: Although it doesn't follow the traditional interview format, this essay by Corso was written in response to questions posed by Howard Nemerov, then Consultant in Poetry to the Library of Congress, to several contemporary poets regarding such subjects as the poetic process and the role of the poet in society. The essay originated as one of a series of Voice of America radio broadcasts in 1964, the transcript of which was published the following year in the collection Contemporary American Poetry.

In his introduction to the 1966 republication of the book,[1] Nemerov wrote, "I proposed four questions to the contributors, explaining, however, that these were to be taken mainly as stimulus or even irritant and need not be regarded at all if the writer's interests took him along some other path. As I might have expected, few set themselves to answer directly; some paid the questions no heed whatever; whereas others, perhaps a majority, wrote essays in which the substance of the questions is obliquely reflected."

Poetry and the poet are inseparable – I cannot write about poetry without writing about the poet. In fact I, as poet, am the poetry I write. I did not know how to write a poem when I felt I wanted to be a poet. I was thirteen years old and I was alone in the world – no mother, and my father was at war. I belonged to the streets and no school did I attend: to exist I stole minor things and to sleep I slept on the rooftops and in the subways of the city, the big wild city of New York during World War II in 1943. I went through a strange hell that year and I guess it is just such hells that give birth to the poet. There swelled in me at the time some inexpressible joy and sorrow; I wanted to tell the whole world about it, but just didn't know how.

If I had remained on the streets I might not have known how. I was sent to prison. I truly don't feel that my life was ill-directed, if it was I who ill-directed it, and that is sheer nonsense – my direction has always been goodly, no matter what the clime, realm, situation. What would seem to most as a great injustice – being sent to prison in my seventeenth year, where I was the youngest inmate, rather than to a boy's reformatory, if such had to be – proved to be one of the greatest things that ever happened to me.

In prison I was not hampered by the undeveloped and ofttimes silly consciousness of youth; in prison I had to deal with men, all kinds of men, caught in a single fate; and with time, three years of it. In that time I read many great books and spoke to many amazing minds – men who had spent years on Death Row and had been reprieved – one can never forget talking to such souls. One man told me "Boy, don't you serve time, let time serve you." So it did; time, so often so cruel, was kind and beneficial to me. When I left, I left there a young man, educated in the ways of men at their worst and at their best. For this reason I am unable to say anything really bad about prison. I do not say prison is a good place – far from it. For the middle-aged and old, it is a breathing coffin – any door locked against a man is a sad business. But I am me and it is not my fashion to dislike a dislikable thing when that thing has, in its strange way, been beneficial to me. Sometimes hell is a good place – if it proves to one that because it exists, so must its opposite, heaven, exist. And what was that heaven? Poetry.

I did not write poems about prison or prison men. I wrote about the world outside because I was once again outside with the world. I was of the world, not of prison. In prison I only learned, I did not write. If one must climb a ladder to reach a height and from that height see, then it were best to write about what you see and not about how you climbed. Prison to me was such a ladder.

A saving grace and a disturbing handicap it is to speak from the top of your head, putting all trust in your self as truthsayer. I write from the top of my head and to write so means to write honestly, but it almost means to write clumsily. No poet likes to be clumsy. But I decided to heck with it, as long as it allows me to speak the truth. If the poet's mind is shapely then his poem will come out shapely.

My first poem I remember only slightly; I have no copy of it; I lost it with hundreds of others, none of which I remember, in a bus terminal in Miami Beach, Florida, of all places. I had them in a suitcase – that's all I used to carry with me on my frequent itineraries, one big sole suitcase in which I would have a shirt and a suit, all crumpled up, amidst a deluge of poems. I never went back to claim that suitcase. But years later I went to the president of the bus company and he said they had probably been destroyed. So much for my early works. I never felt badly about it because I felt myself to be inexhaustible – like I had a great big supply of this stuff called poetry. The only care I took, and maybe not even that so well, was not to lose the poet. As long as I had the poet I would have the poems.

Even when I traveled throughout Europe during these last five years I still carried with me one suitcase, and still the same contents, fifty poems to one pair of underwear. Many times when passing customs I would have to open my suitcase and all the customs man would see would be poems, poems, poems. Only a diplomat arrives with so many papers – surely by my looks and much traveled-in clothes I looked like no diplomat. So what else could I be but a spy, or a poet, or both. A poet is a spy, but not the political kind. He's everybody's spy, he spies for everybody and reports to everybody. Keats claimed he was God's spy. Since I believe in man, that makes me mankind's spy. Anyway I never really had any trouble with the border customs, except that it was always kind of difficult to close the suitcase. I would have it packed down real tight, so when I had to open it in the train compartment, which was usually crowded, the poems would jump up like a jack-in-the-box and fly everywhichway, which was a kind of drag – so I tried traveling without them and that proved to be not such a good idea because I then lost them; I think I have lost more poems than I have at hand. The best thing that could have happened to me and to the poems was my getting a publisher. As soon as I had finished a batch of them, I would send it off to my New York publisher. In that way the poems were saved.

From the time I was a child to the time I left prison I was a poet, but one who did not write any poems. When I left prison I began to write very much and maybe they were not any good – I'd like to think that was the reason for my losing them. I began to take care not to lose my poems when I wrote less. Somehow I felt, in the beginning, that it was too easy to write poetry; that even though most critics hail poetry as being one of the most difficult arts, I couldn't believe it so. As I say, I found it too easy to write this great big difficult thing. But the time came when I could only write one or two poems a month, a time when it became really hard to put down on paper what I wanted to express from the heart. It is those poems, the ones that took sweat and laborious joy to create, which remain.

The distribution of poetry among poets is a fair distribution; and the understanding of poetry is, today, more distinguished and distributed than ever before. It makes no difference whether a poem is abundantly distributed or not; as long as it holds the truth and power of the poet's advanced consciousness it will, whether understood or not, whether accepted or not, reach the main and general consciousness of mankind in time and thereby benefit it. Such is the poem's magic and this is the true mystery of poetry – its ability to advance and better the lot of men's minds.

There is a reason for the poem, for the poet – just as there was a reason for the navigator-explorer, the sea, the ship, and the discovery. Someone must "Christopher-Columbus" the mind, the great expanse of the consciousness, and this the poet does. But unlike Columbus who discovered a new world, a world that was there, the poet must make a new world – it is not there until he himself puts it there. He must put it there and discover it for all peoples and time. When I have had the self-insight to realize that what I had written was like a key to an unwritten door, I wrote that door, and when I opened it, what lay behind such a door? Nothing. Nothing, unless I put something there. I know that I shall not find anything not for the looking, I know that I must create the room of my truth's desire; and then, and only then, may I enter and dwell in peace and joy. For if the poet is at peace and with joy then, rest assured, all humankind is. But all humankind is not at peace, is not joyous, and never has it been – will it ever be? Can such a humankind come about? I am able to imagine it, but I do not think it is possible. All peoples are not one people. Some will be happy and some will be unhappy, and vice versa. To have the whole world happy and yet have a rope that can hang you ... tells me that as long as there is death there will be unhappiness. Sorrow, like death, is inevitable. This is our fate. As for sorrow, the only thing we can do about it is try to make others happy; and as for death, the only thing we can do about that is to prevent it from going mad. This is the main concern of the poet of today. He has accepted the inevitable. He must now learn how best to live with it.

And yet the comedy is that everyone seems to be living with it with a better heart and spirit than the poet. Such is the case, here in America.

I feel it is a comedy that I am a poet in such a world as the world is today. Even though I feel that words like "modern" and "contemporary" are illusory words and that all peoples are of one time and one spirit, I am left with the odd feeling that in this world a poet may write a perfect poem but he may not perfect himself. He is secondary to the poem. Let the poet suffer, but do not let the poem suffer nor have it suffer us. I say this is a sad comedy because whatever light the poet may have to offer, he – and not the poem –

offers it. The light comes from the poet, not from the poem. The poet gives it to the poem and the poem gives it to man. In America we honor poetry, not poets.

I am the substance of my poetry. If you honor poetry, you honor me; if you damn me, you damn poetry. I am the poetry I write. I live it, joy it, suffer it, and I wish all that is great and wonderful in it for myself and for all, and no poem have I written that was not, in one way or another, akin to me as is my flesh. Everything I know I know from man, and books, and myself – and since books are the issue of man, and since I myself am a man, it then goes to say that the whole business of poetry is in the hands of man. Poetry is nothing without man. The world is a tough place to live in and for the poet it can be unbearable. In all this spin of human endeavor the poet-man is fated to dwell on the outskirts of humankind. The poet more than any other figure in all of human time is the only being unstained by dark, monstrous, unforgivable deeds – and yet he lives as though he were exiled from life by life. It is a lonely, laborious, unrewarding place – that necessary outskirt. No, the poet is not the happiest of people, indeed he could well be the least happy.

I doubt that the poets of yesteryear had as hard and as awkward a time as does the poet today and I doubt the poet today will have had it as hard and as awkward as the poet to come. It is the poet, now, and not the poem, that must become a work of art – that must be lovely and perfect. The times demand that the poet – that is, man – be as true as a poem. And this is happening. Poets are their poems.

I'd say these poets are extremely different from the poets of old, first, because of their stress on the psyche rather than on the poem. They wholly believe that if the poet's being is of a good shape so the poem will be of a good shape. It is impossible for a crooked poet to create a straight poem. And second, the poet today has to cope with a changing world and a changing common consciousness; he has to deal with the unpoetic rather than the poetic; this goes completely contrary to his entire make-up, his whole being; yet he must himself change or else die. He sees the world changing and he realizes he must change with it if he is to survive. This is his new and difficult and heavy state – the process is all too clear: the world is changing therefore man must change, and the poet, who sooner than most becomes aware of the changing, must blow the trumpet.

The poet today does not really want to sing about trees. I once saw myself doting upon tree-poetry with my time; I had to deny such poetry because a far more desperate poetry beckoned. I recall some "nature" poets taunting me with: "But trees are so beautiful and, indeed, far grander than man." I pounded my fist on a wooden table and said: "This is what man does to trees."

Today in America there are many poets; all have something to say, some say it badly and some say it excellently, and yet all speak of love of goodness and of hopes of universal individual freedom; all are indicative of a new consciousness, a new age; they seem to represent both dusk and dawn. Today as in no other time in human history the poet is face to face with the world about him, at times at odds and at times fully with it. He sees himself, and sees how others see him, and both eyes seldom meet. The poet cries for a change in society, not for himself but for all peoples; yet he and not the people is the one in need of the change. There seems to be no society for the poet. In America the poet is something of a joke; and then again, something of a rebel, if he happens to step on an old toe of society. No one owns society and the poet most certainly would be the last to claim to; but he can, more than anyone in that society, bring about a change within it. He can do this, but fate would have it even then that he would be unable to enter that changed society. He is doomed to live on its fringe. The fault lies with no one. The poet is of his own world; it is the best that life can offer him and it should be sufficient – it should be, but it is not.

I feel that in the future many many poets will blossom forth – the poetic spirit will spread and reach toward all; it will show itself not in words – the written poem – but rather in man's being and in the deeds he enacts. If this should come about it will then be necessary for both worlds, the world of the poet and the world that belongs to everybody, to join and become a possibility. A handful of poets in every country in the world can and have always been able to live in the world as well as in their own world; and whether by chance, or by will, or by fate, it was not the people but the poet, who did not wish his world to be infringed upon. But when such humankind becomes manifold, when all are embraced by the poetic spirit, by a world of poets, not by the written word but by deed and thought and beauty, then society will have no recourse but to become suitable for them and for itself. I feel man is headed in such a direction; he is fated and due to become aware of and knowledgeable about his time; his good intelligence and compassion will enable him to cope with almost all the bothersome, distracting difficulties that may arise – and when he becomes so, "poet" will not be his name, but it will be his victory.

Man will change, and so will the poet – he too is in need of change because he too is far from perfect – in fact there are many poets who are downright messes. In America especially – where the poet is more likely to be bereft of respect and honor. Respect and honor is something almost every being wants – indeed, demands. The sad thing about respect and honor in America is that it takes money to have them; therefore the American poet who wishes respect and honor is defeated before he starts, because money is a very difficult thing to obtain, and for a poet it is almost virtually impossible. A fool and his money are soon parted, but a poet and money never even meet to be parted. And that old muse's tale about poets writing better when they are famished and ill-housed is downright idiocy.

I think of the poet because I know full well that the poem is nothing without the poet, that there would be no poetry were there no poets. Everything today seems to work against the poet; he is always in danger of being wiped out. The way the poet is treated today, I doubt that any future poet would want to be a poet – not if he has anything on the ball. First of all, given his extreme sensitivity and even if he is less sensitive, he would not accept the stigma of being classified as some kind of character or rebel because he is a poet. His intelligence would not want the insult of cheap publicity (if he happens to be controversial) – movie stars wish it because it brings them popularity and money. To the poet it brings nothing but destructive popularity without the sad recompense of gold. The poet, unlike the popular star or singer, is not an entertainer. I relate mostly to my own country, America, where I hold that if it were not for poetry, for that generation of poetry that I am a part of, America would be a pretty square business. As it was, it was the poets who took that stifling squareness out of it.

I do not pity the poet of America today or yesterday because if ever there was an American poet's cry, it was never for freedom. The poet in America is free to do anything he can or hopes to regarding the state of poetry and his own state of being a poet. If the poet feels he is in a lousy state then it is up to the poet alone to change that state – not his poetic state, because all the poets of the world and of history have always been free; if a poet needs help in his poetic state then he is alone, nobody can help him. It is in his human state, the poet as a human being, that he may be mixed up and uncertain and ofttimes ill-treated and hurt. The poet does not suffer his poetry, he suffers his humanity – it is his humanity I am concerned with. I feel it is treated ungraciously, stupidly, and sometimes dangerously.

I do not say that if a country does extend respect and honor to its poets that it will have poets. Many countries I have been to, countries known for their respectful treatment of the artist, were clearly lacking in poets. My concern is not just with American poets but with the poets of the world because a poet is first of all a universal being – that is why it is impossible for a true poet to be nationalistic. To write poems for the state and not from his heart is death to the poet.

So I contend that the state of the poet on earth today is lousy. In America he is looked upon as something strangely averse to the American way of life; in Russia he is unable to sing his song – he must sing for the state and no poet can sing a song not his; in Europe he is exhausted; in Asia he doesn't exist; the dark cloud of uncertainty prevails over all. And this necessary agent, once the agent of beauty, is now the recipient of certainty. That is why the poet must be. The world is uncertain; the poet is striving toward certainty.

The world is changing; and what makes for uncertainty is that the world is aware that it is changing. To not know that the world is changing is to be certain of a world, familiar and old, a world that is no longer – the past always seems safer than the future because we know the past; we don't know the future. Gone is the certainty of yesterday's world, a world molded once by new ideas and ways, soon to become familiar and decadent, old and dying. The ideas and ways of yesterday are dead. The world now seems to sit back and to ask: "Okay, now what? What next?" Nobody knows; nobody can know; one can only hope or predict or try to make what is hoped for and predicted a reality. I feel that it takes uncertainty to get to what is certain. A smart man knows that no one can be certain about life, especially the changing life of the present – to be thus certain is to be presumptuous and ill-visioned; it is against the nature of life. Today man is at a level with the world; the world goes on and it needs man to help it go on, not for the world's sake but for man's sake, because the world will always go on – man is the only thing in danger of not continuing. He is stuck in the world; he can't get out without dying, so he is able to take the reins of the world and direct. He has no other choice, if he wants to continue on, that is. And so the world goes on; life goes on and death goes on, and poets come and go, and death comes before life, and poetry comes after life, and everything, yes, everything is changing. Man is changing, seas and mountains are changing, dresses and cars are changing. It has always been so, but it has not always been like it is today. Today we are fully aware of the changing process in and around us – we are close to it, and for the first time in human history we are wholly uncertain of what will come of it all.

The world is getting bigger while getting smaller, as it diminishes via rocket speed it expands via human thought, via our consciousness. There are no more lands to explore, to conquer – Christopher Columbus must now traverse the sea of the mind and who can doubt he'll not discover some kind of wondrous continent there? Once this new mental territory is found and opened up, people will most assuredly migrate there and settle there and build. The wonderful human mind has long ago been to the moon – we are our own rockets; and the bigger the rocket the farther the journey; so the wider the expanse of the mind the greater our possibility to learn and enjoy the adventures it holds for us. But one cannot take this maturing consciousness of peoples for granted. Man still suffers; his compassion, his broken heart cries out "O God" perhaps to no God – man seems to be a god-minded creature without a god. He knows the cause of his uncertain predicament; he knows that it is man who torments man; that it is not life that is bad or sad but man that is bad, sad. All know that it is man who operates the cannon, the viseboot, the electrode; everything imagined about hell is imagined by man; it was man drove the tank, fired the bullet – men are killed more often by men than by anything else. The human plague is always on. It is man who makes death a lousy, stinking business, who makes death fearsome and a sorry thing for all. We must all die but it is how we die that counts. The crowded world clamors for birth control, yet death control seems to be more our fashion. Death has never been the property of man.

We are a great, fast, learning, growing people, and with all the death thrown at us, by us, somehow we manage to strive toward peace with some kind of dignity and love.

So I will conclude with the feeling that the poet today must be unlike the poet; he cannot be a discriminator between heart and soul, flesh and spirit, beauty and ugliness, truth and untruth. He stands merely as a man, a man who feels that he is but the guardian of the human consciousness and that when he dies there will be another poet to take his relay, in order that consciousness grow ever more perfect, and man ever more human, and life ever more total.

CONVERSATION WITH
ALLEN GINSBERG & GREGORY CORSO
David Widgery

The following discussion between Allen Ginsberg, Gregory Corso and U editor David Widgery took place a few days after the poetry reading at the Albert Hall on June 11, 1965.

GINSBERG: At the Albert Hall,[1] poetry covered itself with urine. Would that something beautiful had happened! There was an opportunity there to present the lung-breath of English poetry and the poets were lacking. There were all these second-rate English poets coming on like semantic beatniks.

WIDGERY: (*To Corso*) Why didn't you read properly? You ran away like a kind of crated dehydrated chicken.

CORSO: I did not run away like a crated dehydrated chicken. I ran away as I is and am, by God. No, really I didn't feel it at all that night. It wasn't the audience. I've faced audiences … it was the way the evening was going and I was bugged about it earlier. I thought I'd be reading with poets. None of them were poets but the five Americans. Nationalistic, yes. There are some English poets, but they weren't there.

WIDGERY: But there were 5,000 people there, and it should have happened.

GINSBERG: I, Allen Ginsberg, accept full responsibility …

CORSO: Why are you jumping on me? I was in Paris and I was told to come to the reading at the Albert Hall, and when I thought of the Albert Hall then I said that it's under the auspices of responsible people. It sounded like a responsible business with Neruda, Allen, myself, Ferlinghetti and Fernandez. I thought, wonderful, it's historical. I haven't read in three years and I wasn't going to read again for some time. The new poems I have are not readable aloud. Why couldn't I just read a straight poem that I did …

WIDGERY: But you just sat there and mumbled into the microphone. I couldn't hear you. Why?

CORSO: Why? Because first of all I told you I was dehydrated – no, you said I was dehydrated. The big why is why didn't that reading come out with the poets reading that I thought would be reading when I came here to London.

WIDGERY: Why didn't Voznesensky read?

CORSO: Because it was a big hodgepodge of a nightmare. He was sitting there watching it … the madness going on there, the nightmare. He saw some very strange scenes outside of the poetry. Perhaps that's why he didn't get up and read.

But today he did. When he saw that the poetry was there and that the poets were giving out with the poetry, he could feel it. And he read in Russian and the people felt the poem. He did not have a translator for today. They felt it and it was real.

WIDGERY: But this means poetry is a kind of silent cinema … words have no meaning.

CORSO: No! The sound … the rhythm and the sound. Words have meaning, because he gave a literal translation, which is the best you can give. Why have a translation into Russian? In English it's just not like the Russian. Voznesensky himself speaks English a little, so he gives you a literal translation and then reads the poem which is much finer.

GINSBERG: Because he reads poems with a fantastic rhythm. A great Kremlin Bell sound that came forth from the belly.

WIDGERY: But why does this happen for 200 people and not for 5,000?

CORSO: Because of the people reading that night. It was disorganised. It had nothing to do with the crowd. You said that 5,000 is better to relate to than 200. I don't know too much about that, but I came here believing that five people would read and it seemed that 15 people read, and there wasn't enough time to go around.

WIDGERY: That was a terrible end, with voices booming out saying, "Go back to your homes, if you have any."

CORSO: They did four hours and it was right for them to say anything if they felt that they did not get anything out of it. You should have had an organiser who would have known just what poets would be there and it would not have been still or awkward like that, but a beautiful reading, by everyone being [in] rapport with it. But you just have one clown get up there … the guy who started the evening was clowning, so that was the keynote for the nightmare. So I looked at it later and said, "Oh hell, it's happened." Looked at it objectively it's almost a comical thing. That's what they came for maybe, and that's what they got.

That was the first reading ever in my life that I read like that. Allen knows how I used to read … I used to go with it, and read poems that related to the audience. That's why my head was bowed, reading my poem[2] mainly to myself and to the poets in the circle. It could have been saved.

AN INTERVIEW WITH GREGORY CORSO
Michael Andre

INTRODUCTORY SHOT

Kirby Congdon, in his introduction to Corso's recent *Dear Fathers*,[1] describes him as "the most important poet of the Fifties." This leads to a question: what happened in the Sixties? And the questionable – those things crotchety Fifties critics disliked – remains. In the interview, Corso answers many of the questions. Here, I will try to set up a preliminary context, both to introduce the interview and Corso's achievement.

"Corso, by some definitions, may not yet even be technically a poet." Richard Brukenfeld defended Corso's first book against critics by whose definition Corso was soon less a poet. Like Breton and the surrealists, Corso writes, often, a spontaneous poetry. In introducing his second book, Corso uses the analogy of jazz –

> When Bird Parker or Miles Davis blow a standard piece of music, they break off into their own-self little unstandard sounds – well, that's the way with my poetry … Of course many will say a poem written on that order is unpolished, etc. – that's just what I want them to be – because I have made them truly my own – which is inevitably something NEW – like all good spontaneous jazz, newness is accepted and expected.

One context would be the Fifties' debates on "conformity"; but artistically both the surrealist precedent and the analogy of jazz are misleading. Corso identifies, in such poems as "Mexican Impressions" and "Early Morning Writings," with the impressionists. I would suggest impressionism as a better precedent and analogy for his writing, which, as he says in the interview, is less "spontaneous" in the manner of Kerouac or Breton than "rapid." Painters have always sketched; the impressionist originality was in rejecting the time-consuming studio masterpiece for this "painted sketch." Corso broke with the rhymed, metered "square" poems of both Tate and Ransom and the British after Auden.

Corso regards much of his work as prophecy. How curiously this relates to scholarship, the resolute study of the past; but it is merely the root meaning of "avant-garde." Until the *ancient/moderne* controversy of the seventeenth century, Western literature in its "highest" forms dealt, like scholarship, with the past. The realist originality, as Linda Nochlin points out, was an emphasis on the "present": beginning with Stendhal and Daumier, art in its highest forms, not only satire and polemic, became critique of society. The "avant-garde" originality was a new separation of the artist from society so that the artist could experiment and offer society new alternatives.

Poetry has many "guards" of course, all regarding themselves as advance. Two of Corso's long new poems, "Mutation of the Spirit" and "Eleven Times a Poem," assault the Aristotelian notions of beginning, middle and end; they are sequences that yet repudiate, like Cage, developmental. "Ethnopoetics," a partially anthropological restatement of primitive or esoteric cultures by Schwerner, Tarn, and Rothenberg, would include another new piece, "The Geometric Poem." His early comic work was linked for praise with Koch's as "late beat" by Michael Benedikt, whose own work, with Erica Jong's, I would call late counter-culture comic. Corso is of the avant-garde. But his relation to the other members is always special. The literary avant-garde, even when comic, resembles some massive post-doctoral program in the creative arts. All the ethnopoetic people have graduate training, as do the leaders of the New York School, Benedikt, Jong, and even the major beats Ginsberg, Ferlinghetti, Snyder, Creeley and Burroughs. But Corso has less education than Le Douanier, Henri Rousseau.

It is difficult to recall a single creative artist of the twentieth century who does not, in some way, claim the "primordial." But Corso is naive or primitive in the technical sense of Oto Bihalji-Merin's *Modem Primitives: Masters of Naive Painting*. To embody his dream landscapes, Henri Rousseau went, naively, to the Jardin des Plantes and painted what he saw. Corso, in the interview, says zoos, with museums, are main sources. Bringing the mandrill into the bedroom can be equated with bringing Jadwiga's couch to the jungle.

Ginsberg's "The Lion is for Real" probably derives from such Corso poems. Neither Rousseau nor Corso are willing to be conventional artists. Because he was incapable of perspective or "tactile" drawing, Rousseau suggested much to cubists and surrealists. Corso, as we have seen, is within the avant-garde; but stylistically, of even the advanced "Mutation of the Spirit," he denies the influence of the other members, in this case, Cage. Corso's free verse is free of Mr. Olson's confining elaboration. "I never pondered too deeply on that."

Like Rousseau, and as in *Lear*, Corso is our "fool." Notice how often in the interview he describes humor as his sole political tool. Yet "Power," "Mutation of the Spirit," "Geometric Poem" are a wisdom literature. The anticipations of cubism and surrealism in Rousseau were similarly less goofy than visionary. Corso's persona, as distinct from its activity, appears fully described only once, in "Clown" –

> It is time for the idiot
> to pose a grin and foot on the dead lion
> (the embodiment of the clownless man) –
>
> ...
>
> No, I shan't crowd your brainy grave;
> it's enough I climb your jolly ladder
> and have planets kick dust in my eyes.
>
> ...
>
> And why do they say be a man, and not a clown?
> And what is it like to be a man?

Corso is Ginsberg's ignu.[2]

Much of Corso begins in laughing critique of society. "Marriage" and "Suburbia Mad Song" butcher, humorously, notions of courtship and marriage. "Three Loves" narrates the kinds of sorrow consequent to a renunciation of patience and fidelity. "The Love of Two Seasons," weaker than these other poems, curiously wraps love in a fairy tale atmosphere:

> When once in wildhood times
> I'd aerial laughter my mischief
>
> When once she opened her arms
> and held me with excited tenderness

Corso even fails to address the poem, one of his few love poems, to the woman, but instead to an imagined child-like audience. "Sura" and "Ode to Sura" do use the second person singular address; Sura, as Corso says in the interview, was one of the very few early beat women, and consequently agreed with his critique of society.

> Not the fly with your magnitude wonder why.
> Yourself wonder but with silence and sly.
> Watch you move from pot to pan – don't cry.
> No thing can ever break your heart.
> When your dreams are fullest the cruel hammer will blow
> And die at your heart.
>
> Too late! The sky is brown.

But the relation, and these lines are typical, was massively and mutually destructive.

"Police" and "Army" offer a critique of coercive authority in society much like "Marriage." At times, Corso can involve authority in his own warped gentleness:

Second Night in N.Y.C. After 3 Years

> I was happy I was bubbly drunk
> The street was dark
> I waved to a young policeman
> He smiled
> I went up to him and like a flood of gold
> Told him all about my prison youth
> About how noble and great the convicts were
> And about how I just returned from Europe
> Which wasn't half as enlightening as prison
> And he listened attentively I told no lie
> Everything was truth and humor
> He laughed
> He laughed
> And it made me so happy I said:
> "Absolve it all, kiss me!"

"No no no no!" he said
and hurried away.

"I depend on heroes for opinion and acceptance," he says in the poem "Power";
notice how beautifully child-like he is, even in asserting the nobility of crime.

How powerless I am in playgrounds
Swings like witches woosh about me

Still linked to childhood, the opening of "Police," "On the Death of the Lucky
Gent" and "Beyond Delinquency" describe with delight anti-social
criminality; to Michael Horovitz, Corso is a lovably American gangster; but
then, Corso did spend three years in prison.

The child's point of view is probably Corso's commonest theme.
Compensating for the poems of juvenile delinquency, there are the visionary
poems; "No Doubt What He Saw" and "The Mad Yak" combine the child's
point of view and the theme of animals. The yak is speaking:

That tall monk there, loading my uncle,
   he has a new cap.
And that idiot student of his –
   I never saw that muffler before.
Poor uncle, he lets them load him.
How sad he is, how tired!
I wonder what they'll do with his bones?
And that beautiful tail!
How many shoelaces will they make of that!

Similarly exotic, "The French Boy's Sunday" takes its charm from the
speaker's use of a formal pseudo-translated "we"; Ashbery with "you" and
Creeley and Mailer with "he" have recently used similar pronoun masks. "The
Last Warmth of Arnold" is a veiled funky little tale about a boy who dies,
c. 1940, sniffing glue. Other poems such as "Doll Poem" live among the toys
and symbols of childhood; but Corso's identification with the child, which
seems angelic in "Second Night in N.Y.C.," constantly breaks down into
something more adult, or at least more violent:

Confused I'd best leave wonder and candy and school
and go find amid ruin the peremptory corsair.[3]

"The great act" is Corso's theme, latent in most poems, even the poems of childhood, even the anthropological poems. He attempts to revivify greatness. Perceval, at least as Chrétien de Troyes portrays him, begins as a fool nursed by only one parent, but, because of a capacity for growth which is ever in Perceval (and Corso) he evolves into the only visionary hero in the Arthurian tales. It's a question now if his vision, in this period, is of unrelenting negation or not. "Mutation of the Spirit" is a farewell to a golden age and I am frightened to think that to Corso my present is his past, his golden age.

> As a child I saw many things I did not want to be.
> Am I the person I did not want to be?
> The talks-to-himself person?
> The neighbors-make-fun-of person?
> Am I he who, on museum steps, sleeps on his side?
> Do I wear the cloth of a man who has failed?
> Am I the looney man?
> In the great serenade of things,
>   am I the most cancelled passage?[4]

Corso's is an imagination locked into tunnels talking to itself. "What is he saying?" Ginsberg asks in the introduction, and answers "Who cares?!" He also says Corso is "probably the greatest poet in America."

Michael Andre

THE INTERVIEW

4:00 p.m.

ANDRE: In your poem "The American Way" you wrote:

> And those who seek to get out of the Way
>   can not
> The Beats are good example of this
> They forsake the Way's habits
>   and acquire for themselves their own habits
> And they become as distinct and regimented and lost

as the main flow
because the Way has many outlets
like a snake of many tentacles –
There is no getting out of the Way
The only way out is the death of the Way
And what will kill the Way but a new consciousness

You wrote that in 1961. Do you have a different perspective on that now after eleven years?

CORSO: I think always in the beginning of something things look very similar, but then they do disperse. They depicted the beats of the time with bangles and shaggy hair; long and shaggy hair and beards. But not so much the look. I didn't mean regimentation by look so much as a particular way, their way. I was very much hung up on individualism at the time. I still am. People who have a particular connection with their ideas, the poets that I knew, the beats that I really knew, Kerouac, Ginsberg, Burroughs, they were all very diverse in their writing styles, but there was a similarity through it with their feeling of what was coming, of what was to be. I think that Kerouac with his whole Beat Generation thing was just a prophecy of what would be. The generation is not just for writers, you know; it pertains to the mass, and that was not there at the time. It was just little pockets in North Beach and in Greenwich Village at the time. By 1961, of course, the beats were passing, and there's the hip thing starting to spread out more and more, and that's the thing, I think, that I was seeing at the time. They were diverse.

I think in that poem I state that the young also were hampered, were not doing anything, "but not for long." I put in parentheses there "but not for long." And that came to be, they did do something.

That poem and "America Politica Historia" – the publisher really goofed on that; I told him to put the date on it. It was published in 1959. I think when people read it they can see that it must have been written a long time ago. It couldn't be written now. But it states in there that Nixon would be the last president. There is a question mark there though. I ask, will he be the last president? That's a premature long shot, because he was just going against Kennedy then, right?

ANDRE: Yes.

CORSO: Now all right, so Kennedy beats him, so that would knock him out, you know, the last president thing, and when you think of Bobby Kennedy afterwards and all that, this man would have no chance, and would be losing in California, but there he is, right back there!

It's very hard for me to write political poems. Humor is one form I love. It's a butcher in a way, it gets rid of a lot of shit. But it's very, very hard today to write anything humorous about the Vietnam War. How can you be funny about that? (*Pause*)

ANDRE: Have you been writing much lately?

CORSO: Yes.

ANDRE: What have you been writing?

CORSO: The scene, the big scene mainly, that I got onto in the late Fifties was death; it was the atom bomb, ban the bomb, and all. Then in the Sixties came two other big words that were taken care of – Love and God. God is Love, or Love is God, the flower children and what not. There's two more big ones handled. When we come to the Seventies I figured the big daddy would be Truth.

ANDRE: Talking about Truth in our society, and the difficulties that we unlike the Greeks and Romans have dealing with it, you asked in "1959," "must I dry my inspiration on this sad concept?" Were you afraid that that might happen?

CORSO: It did happen. I found that going back to Greece I was no longer awestruck by looking at the Acropolis and things like that. I think that's what gave me my opening when I was a kid, to see something in books, you know, pictures, of beautiful old stone and what not.

The literature and the mythologies of ancient times grabbed me, but today no, it's more held down to what is going on, the present day. But I think it's no longer a sad thing. It's just a change of feeling I knew would happen.

ANDRE: That's interesting. Allen Ginsberg and I spent a long time trying to find the meaning of the word *classicist*, and we decided that it was someone who found great value in past civilizations, particularly Greece and Rome. Would you say you are a classicist?

CORSO: Well, I could say I was. And I could say I still retain it because it's all in my head. I mean, if anyone were to ask me about Carthage or Phoenicia, or about the Bogomils or about the Sumer and *Gilgamesh*, I know the shot.

But other things are more pressing today. I still incorporate that in my poetry at times; it's occasional, you know, it's like an encyclopedic hold in my head that I can at times pick on and use.

I knew the change was coming in that poem. It was 1959, and I knew the change would occur. That's why I ended the book with the poem.

ANDRE: I noticed in *The Vestal Lady on Brattle* you don't use the exploded, fragmentary line of your later poems, such as "Bomb."

CORSO: Right.

ANDRE: Was that "projective verse?"

CORSO: I didn't know anything about projective verse, Mr. Olson and the Black Mountain[5] people, until Ginsberg introduced me to it – and when the heck was that? That was pretty much late. No, I never pondered too deeply on that. The first book, it's very awkward, a green book, just ideas trying to come out. Lots of imagery, conglommed together; and I cut out lots of fat. I thought in those days that poetry is a concise form, built like a brick acropolis; but in 1957–58 in Paris things burst and opened, and I said, "I will just let the lines go and not care about fat." I figured if I could just go with the rhythm I have within me, my own sound, that that would work, and it worked. In "Marriage" there was hardly any change – there are long lines, but they just flow, like a musical thing within me. I could do that much better than so-called eye forms, forms that you could see with your eye.

Most of the poems I write are not written for oral reading. Take a guy like Ferlinghetti; he would know that he has to read his poems aloud; that would be with the measured thing, the projective thing. They set it down on paper the way they speak. Mine is written the way I felt within me. It's difficult to get up and read them, because it isn't meant for that. I mean, you could read faster on paper than aloud.

ANDRE: In your first work there are many little anecdotes, little observations, little scenes, for instance "St. Lukes, Service for Thomas" and "The Greenwich Village Suicide" from *Vestal Lady on Brattle*.

CORSO: Well, yes, that's observing a little scene, and setting it down as such.

I think *Gasoline* has a lot of that in it, but *Gasoline* is a change. You can see the change coming in *Gasoline*, where I would take a jump, and make an elliptical shot. I juxtapose lots of images together. I see two gangsters on the street, "... guns rusting in their hands." The observance of *Gasoline* was inward, except maybe for the zoo poems, where I did observe literally, like:

> In the Mexican Zoo
>   they have ordinary
> American cows.[6]

ANDRE: *Elegiac Feelings American* has a lot of dense, grammatically complex poems. That was another change.

CORSO: Yes, that was another change. That's the last. Now I've learned to not use words I could use very freely, like the word God, the word man, which I hate to be so free using now, what with women's lib and all.

ANDRE: You also started revising poems. There is one poem in particular, "Ode to Myself and Her" which you changed to "Ode to Sura." I don't know what "Sura" means.

CORSO: Oh, that was the girl, that was "her," you see. I must have had it published twice in a magazine. There is also a poem in the *Elegiac* that the publisher didn't know was already published in *Gasoline*, but it's a different version.

ANDRE: Yes, "Hedgeville" I think.

CORSO: Right. That was found in an earlier magazine. If they are already published, I don't correct anymore, although sometimes I am really tempted to. I know I could clean out a lot of them, and really set them aright, but then I let them go, and I don't bother. I usually correct poetry at the time I'm working on it. Usually it's elimination rather than augmenting.

ANDRE: Auden revises all the time.

CORSO: Yes, that one could do. I see it in a very funny way. If it's already out – you see, like the thing that would disturb me in the *Elegiac* was that the publisher did not put the date on a particular poem. Not all my poems are dated, they don't have to be dated, but certain ones had to. So that sort of change I would make.

ANDRE: You use a large vocabulary in your poetry.

CORSO: My vocabulary that I obtained was from a standard dictionary of 1905, that big, when I was in prison. For three lucky years I just got that whole book in me, all the obsolete and archaic words. And through that I knew that I was in love with language and vocabulary, because the words and the way they looked to me, the way they sounded, and what they meant, how they were defined and all that, I tried to revive them, and I did.

ANDRE: What's "dactho"?

CORSO: It's a pesticide, and it sounds very deadly. I also like changing words around, or adding things to words that you won't find in the dictionary, like "miracling."

ANDRE: Or "flowerian" in "Of One Month's Reading of English Newspapers."

CORSO: Yes. That's the one poem where I did have another chance with a word – vagina. I didn't like the sound of vagina, but also there was a little girl that was there fucking dead, and I would say that she was a virgin, therefore say not Virginia, but Virgina. How did I have it? V.I.R.G.I.N.A. Yes, Virgina. There you go. It was a flowery dress, right? "Deathicle" was one. Not many words you can play around with death on.

ANDRE: What's an "exist self"?

CORSO: Pardon?

ANDRE: Oh dear. In *American Express* Frump intercepts a letter for Hinderov mentioning exist-elves, and Frump goes about making an idiot of himself asking people what they are.

CORSO: That book was written in one month, and it's the one I hate because I really did a fast job on that. It's written so awkwardly, I would love to have worked on that one.

ANDRE: I really love it. It's out of print, too. Is there any possibility of getting it printed again?[7]

CORSO: I've been asked. Syntactically and grammatically it's fucked up. That's what I'm getting at. It's not so much the theme, you know. Too many "he says" and "she says." I should know how best to cut that kind of thing out, and just know how the dialogue flows. I could do it in a play fine. Did you ever read my play *In This Hung-up Age*?

ANDRE: No. I didn't know it was a play. I thought it was just a poem.

CORSO: It's a play and it was put on at Harvard in 1954, and in it it has a hipster, it has a square, it has a college girl, it has Mrs. Kindhead, who is one of the girls on demonstrations and all that, it has an Apache Indian as a philosopher in it but a lot of buffalos run him over. He's on the bus going to California, San Francisco, for poetry and jazz. That was a nice little, you know, futuristic look out for something. It was in *Encounter 100* and *New Directions*.

ANDRE: Was the organization of "Mutation of the Spirit" influenced by John Cage[8] and his experiments with chance?

CORSO: No, that was a series of poems that I wrote when I took heroin. I knew that there was a change coming over men, not only the, oh, Catholic thing, the guilt if you are going to take a shot, you know, and you die with it, and look, a poet dead, and all these kids in school and what not, hippies, and there you are, and as an example you are dead with a needle. It wasn't that so much as realizing we are chemical beings, that the body is chemical, and taking in a chemical, how it would change me, you know. So I started writing when I sensed the change. Something was going. It was no longer this. Even though I had come out of prison and had all that wild life before me there was not much change in me; I was still this wild, crazy self. But having taken that shot I figured that a change was there, it was happening chemical-wise. And so when I wrote the poem, I wrote them in two days.

ANDRE: Really? I would have thought it had taken you months and months!

CORSO: I wrote them in two days, and I did not know when I came off the stuff – plus the speed at the time, taking both chemicals, experimenting with both, that was a major experiment. Most of the things I had written were done without taking anything, like *The Vestal Lady, Gasoline, Happy Birthday, Long Live Man*. But that was still when everybody was jumping on the bandwagon taking drugs, and so it was like awkward and I said, "What the Hell, poets do have some kind of old tradition that they can fuck around with this stuff and know how to handle it."

ANDRE: What year was that?

CORSO: In 1964 –1965. So I called that the "Shuffle Poem," meaning that I don't know exactly where you begin or end with this thing, and you can read any page, but it is one poem nonetheless. I have my notebooks, and sometimes it's just like that. I call it a mind now. To have to type them out and make each a separate poem, it really strikes me now as not it. My next book will be very different, like it was written down.

A lot was changing in '64. The bombs were falling down, the whole thing with Vietnam was starting, Kennedy was dead, there was this slow, gradual coming to what you've got today. Which is: One Big Suck. That's what the whole thing is. Everything just went tumbling. Haven't seen anything built up.

And I figured I was a weathervane for what was going down. If things were fucked up then I would be. Now that was a departure; if the world is rational, usually the poet is irrational, and when the world is irrational, then the poet is rational. My friend, beautiful Ginsberg, is rational; when this world is irrational, he is very rational. I can get something out of it – the direction of what's happening.

ANDRE: One of the questions I was going to ask you was about your elegy for the Indians. You were interested in the same thing that, say, Gary Snyder and Allen are interested in.

CORSO: Yes.

ANDRE: But you handle it in a completely different way. You just elegize them and describe them today, rather than attempt to revivify their whole value system.

CORSO: Yes. Now there you go. I wrote that Indian thing very early, in 1958. That was not done when the Indians started, you know – the opening up with the Blacks and civil rights. The feeling was the loss, and I still feel that today. Of course they didn't build the nation, but the land that they did have and the life they did have is gone. There are the hippies and the new Indians, but it will never be the same. It's changed. I look upon it as a stain. This Vietnam War is a stain on this country, so it's a big weight, and I think that's what's hitting people a lot today, whether they know it or not – the inertia, the indifference.

ANDRE: One thing that was similar – let's see if I can phrase this – I asked Allen about his mother's insanity, and he blamed that on the political state of America, and I thought it was interesting that you blamed Jack Kerouac's problems on the state of America.

CORSO: Oh sure, of course, because these are weathervanes. Any voice that comes out seeing something, a vision of what can be, and it's such a beautiful one, well, the tide usually will run against them and do them in. You can't change it, somehow. I held on to Bob Dylan about his "George Jackson."[9] "Why didn't you look at it beforehand, not saying with an elegy how much you loved the man, instead of beforehand doing something?" There is nothing I could do for the Indians before they went, although there are nine million Indians today, they say, the same as there was when the white man first came to this country.

ANDRE: Really?

CORSO: Less buffalo, of course, but the same number of Indians. The genocide wasn't exactly genocide. It was the genocide of taking their land.

ANDRE: Another thing that struck me with "Elegiac Feelings American" as kind of delightful was that you dedicated it "to the dear memory of John Kerouac."

CORSO: Yes.

ANDRE: Which I thought was a kind of Shelleyesque allusion to John Keats, or was that in my imagination?

CORSO: Jack is John, John is Jack. John would be the endearment, whereas usually Jack would be the endearment. I think I made a mistake in that poem. Do you have the book?

>   Pitt Jr. obtained most of
> the city of brotherly love by so outrageous a
> deception as stymied the trusting heart of his
> red brother with torturous mistrust

It wasn't Pitt, it must have been Penn. The Indians told him he could have as much land as he could walk over in a day. So this guy gets three guys who look like him, and they ran like mad. One guy drowned in a stream. And so the Indian says, "They no stopping to eat 'em, they no stopping to shit 'em, they no stopping to smoke 'em, all they do is lun, lun, lun." And that's how they got the city of brotherly love. But I don't think it was Pitt Junior. It must have been Penn Junior or something, you know.

ANDRE: You've written a couple of poems that seem to be an inversion of the theme of "Wichita Vortex Sutra" [by Allen Ginsberg] such as "Death of 1959," "History is Ended," and the character, in fact, of Mr. D. in your novel.

CORSO: If it's in connection with what Allen did, then I would say, when did he do that?

ANDRE: I just mean you were both dealing with the same theme.

CORSO: Okay, that's clear. "Death of 1959" was a cut-up poem. I had maybe three or four pages and I cut it up. I like working with Burroughs. Say, here is a book of Rimbaud, cut it up and make your own, make a million Rimbauds. You have to see what you've got when you pick up the thing, you have to see if wow, does it look great, by that accident of cutting, and *then* put it down. There was a lot that I didn't put in. I wasn't able to put the whole shot in. I picked out what was good. It sounded very much like the poem it was anyway.

ANDRE: What do you mean?

CORSO: Well, as I wrote the poem itself without being cut up; I just shortened the sentences, that's all, and it gave it a different kind of sound, it gave it like a very far out spatial sound.
　　"Air is to Go" was mainly conversation that I had in Tangiers with a particular Arab who told me about tapping shoulders, the "Arab tap-of-shoulder," whereby you know that the space you had is no longer allotted you, and the space that you have has only room for one, for yourself. Once you

give that up you are out, whereas time, you can give time, but you can't give space.

ANDRE: Mr. D. wants to destroy the world by destroying language, and Allen suggested that the way to end the war, in "Wichita Vortex Sutra," was to improve the language.

CORSO: Look, Mr. D. would be, except for the color, Burroughs. Mr. D. is in "The Death of 1959," too. I end up telling Burroughs, "Well, you can't destroy language, you are only going to add to it." Poetry, language, when you attempt to destroy them you just augment them, you are just adding to it. Anything destroyed has got to be with humor. As I say humor is that kind of butcher, but I think a very good one because it surely gets rid of the shit. You know, if you can really laugh at something, especially the way the American mentality used to be, then it was out. You could see the truth through it, if it was laughable, and it is out. About today I don't know.

ANDRE: Another thing – a parallel between your poetry and your novel – "Bomb" struck me as peculiar. It didn't strike me that you just hit at the Bomb. Hinderov in *American Express* loves bombs.

CORSO: "Bomb" was written when I came back from England, when I saw the kids Ban the Bomb, Ban the Bomb, and I said, "It's a death shot that's laid on them, the immediacy of people being hanged in England at that time, and it's not as if the Bomb had never fallen, so how am I going to tackle this thing? Suddenly death was the big shot to handle, Gregory, not just the Bomb."

The best way to get out of it was make it lyrical, like an embracing of it, put all the energy of all the lyric that I could name. And then get to know it. But if I start with hating it, with the hate of it, I get no farther than a piece of polemic, a political poem – which I usually fall flat on. That's not a political poem exactly, that "Bomb" poem. And you can only do it by embracing it, yes. So, gee, I loved the bomb.

Now Hinderov is one of the many characters in that book who has antagonists, he has people against him, right? That person exists all the time, that Hinderov. Look at the bombs falling today, and people condoning it. In 1972, right this day, they are indifferent, and where are those demonstrators now, to cause the disruptions that they do?

Just think of the Miami Convention. They were all asleep, they were all on Quaalude probably. Nixon probably laid that Quaalude on them, that's a sleeper, that's what it is, Quaalude.

ANDRE: Quaalude?

CORSO: Oh man, that's what most of them are taking.

ANDRE: What is it? I don't know what it is.

CORSO: It's a weird pill, just makes you flow along, but not very much fire coming out of you, you know?

ANDRE: I'd never heard of it before.

CORSO: It's a funny thing; it sounds like science fiction but I don't think it is. If you can lay these things on the market – these drugs and what not – and know that the young partake of them, and the word of mouth goes very fast about them, zap, you quiet them down.

ANDRE: Wolfherald in your novel says, "I have always believed in the gift of vision." Do you believe in it too?

CORSO: Oh yes, very much so. I've seen it myself.

ANDRE: Yes?

CORSO: Sure. I can say I can look ahead, you know. Not great big shots in the dark, like sitting there and wow, I had this great big vision that unfolded before my eyes. Not like that. Well, vision is seeing, isn't it? It's just a little more than observing. Seeing, observing, vision. It's a step.

ANDRE: I was thinking of Carrol's[10] vision in the book of the supernatural.

CORSO: His vision was to bring the bad forces into the hands of the good and get it all squared away. You know, that constant battle till today – Satan, the forces that are good. I don't think they are that good anymore. In the Bible, the Sons of God came down and made it with the Daughters of Man. Sounds like space astronauts coming down and injecting them with their megagalactic semen. In other words, who were the Daughters of Man? The form was no longer a dinosaur or fishlike, but apelike, and the two combining made it what is called Man. The missing link was brain. All these anthropologists looking for skulls, and it was a brain change, it wasn't a skull change.

Between ape man and primitive man, that's where morning glory seeds came into being. Through Carbon 14, they can check out the plant life of the time. Plants were divisional before man came. They were born of themselves, no seeds. This is how I checked it out. I said, Well look, if that's morning glory seed, and they do get zapped on that, then all the seed families would have zapped their heads.

ANDRE: That's terrific. What an idea!

CORSO: It's I good one, in the sense that the brain doesn't petrify, so they can't find the connect. I mean it's a theory as good as any other. That could be a vision.

ANDRE: Sure, I would say so.

CORSO: You meant vision in the holy sense. I don't see it that way. For Instance, I look at the stars and I say to myself, "I have no one to thank for those fuckers, no one." I don't look at them and see how beautiful they are and say, "Thank God for this glory," and all, you know? No.

ANDRE: In "Eleven Times a Poem" you speak of the wisest man on earth. Was that Socrates?

CORSO: Right. Piraeus, the man from Piraeus. It's a kind of visionary poem – the man with the antlers.

ANDRE: Right! That was very interesting.

CORSO: Ohhh! Ohhh! It's a dream I had. I think it was the most beautiful dream I ever did have. I came out of a beautiful green wood with brown trees and all, and saw him

> ... godtall and antlered
> He lifts his branched horns from his head like a hat
> and
> hammers them to a tree ... telling me:

> Not until the deer returns
> will everything be all right

I don't know what that meant exactly, maybe because the myth should be ended, and one should get back to the animal stage. The antlered man is a very old, old thing. He is in the first drawings in the most inaccessible parts of caves with bisons and mammoths and mastodons. Have you been to the caves?

ANDRE: No.

CORSO: Oh man, I've been there, and it's fantastic. In the most inaccessible parts, the Shaman liked to fire at night, and you see all these spearholes in these animals, painted on the wall. They are very hazy, right? The coloring and all that. When the fire goes they are like moving on the wall. They kill the animal before they kill it. Indirectly.

So he was depicted on the wall, and that's in the cave at Trois Frères,[11] the Three Brothers.

ANDRE: And your "Geometric Poem" – what were your sources?

CORSO: I was in Paris in 1965, and in a beautiful room on Monsieur le Prince, where Rimbaud lived; it's really nice, a nice little hotel room. All winter, I'd only go out to get my food and my junk, my dope, and back into that room. I had a big book on hieroglyphics and studied geometry; I had a compass. I put the two together because ancient Egypt was very geometrical.

As you can see they are just mostly work papers. I never thought to put it into any kind of form as in a poem. When that was first published in Italy, it was done on big paper, beautiful, but the way he published it here, it was just too condensed. He should have put it down as a separate thing. It's very hard to read.

ANDRE: How is the Egyptian written character as a medium for poetry?

CORSO: You see, I go backwards, like to Greece, right? Ancient Greece and Rome, and I go to Egypt, and from there to Sumer and wedges. I wanted to check into that because people say, they don't know what the ankh is, the symbol of life which Isis holds. I found out what it was and it blows their minds when I tell them. The Egyptians used everything they could see; in other words, there was no abstract symbol. The ankh is a sandal strap; the big toe goes through that hole. (*Laughter*)

I loved the idea of ancient Egypt. You see, 4000 years, they were hung up on the same shot, those people. Four thou! And they never got out of it! Can you imagine? (*Laughs*)

ANDRE: Are there any poems in hieroglyphics or do we know?

CORSO: Well, there's the number. Now what do you think of that one that I transliterated; that sounds like a poem. Here, I'll read it to you.

> My powers have been given me that you may benefit by
> them
> I have raised up constructions which were destroyed at
> their foundations
> Walls without floors, halls without doors
> I gave remedy for every limb
> unjointed, resuscitated the sense
> when all taste was gone
> that the organs benefit by them.

Then I break away from the poem and rap about Johnson with the bombs going down on Vietnam. I get right off that into what was happening during the day.

That's the kind of work I enjoy doing. I really get interested. When I was in Milan, I was stuck on da Vinci. I lived right across the street from Sta. Maria Grazia where the "Last Supper" is. I lived there three months. Every day I'd go into that church and study. I caught what he did. It was a whole geometrical number. Christ sits as a triangle, behind him is a circular window with a square frame. So there's triangle, circle and square.

ANDRE: That's just like Egypt.

CORSO: Right, right. The thing that got me was, you can't see the feet of Jesu. It was there but Napoleon's army came through and broke the door down where the feet were. So I never knew if the feet criss-crossed or were Egyptian. DaVinci was real shot into magic with geometry.

(*For a few minutes Corso instructs Andre in the relations between geometry, the atom bomb, da Vinci, Early Italian geometers, etc., using scraps of paper since lost.*)

So I did my studies pretty well, as I say. The geometry thing, not through school; I only went to the sixth grade. In that sense, I never went to study geometry or trigonometry or algebra and the other shot of languages. Now I can speak French, Italian, Greek when I'm there and put up to it. What I can do is that Egyptian. Cuneiforms don't move me. The Sumerians wrote the first books, before the Egyptians; *Gilgamesh* was the first thing written down. You know why it's important to me? Because I like to go back to the sources. The way I learned that was through Tibetan. When you're dying, they say, if you're conscious, try to think back where that womb came from? That's why I got to the missing link; when the seed family came into being, it touches down into that time. No, nothing conjecture, nothing like science fiction. Tried to get as much as I can that has truth in it. That's why I know all about the caves, see? It's mainly to go back to the sources.

So with all that studying, eventually you'll get into poetry, and you'll have a book. You see, I couldn't have just sat down when I last wrote a book and just continue. I had to replenish. That's what writing an epic would be. You'd have to have an encyclopedic head and set it down.

ANDRE: You've thought of writing an epic?

CORSO: Oh that's always been my little desire. To get some epical shot down.

ANDRE: You are now 42. Are you an old poet man?

CORSO: That's one poem ("I Am 25") I was playing games with. I was struck by the young romantic thing that you should never retract. The changing of poems is not retraction unless you change your feeling, your idea. I have to chalk it up to just my wild, impetuous self in those days, because I don't want to hate anybody. "The old poetmen." What the hell is that? I considered myself an old man a long, long time ago, maybe when I came out of prison when I was 20 years old, and there was a lot of fire in me still. Can't put any time on that.

ANDRE: Another old poem I was going to ask you about is "Marriage." You got married.

CORSO: I was not wise enough to check out my own poem to help me out. I had to go and fuck up to find out. The kid was born, which is beautiful. Now I realize I haven't had the baby or the woman I love, and no marriage was needed. (*Laughs*) They still got my name, so what the heck. I had to learn, you see. That's the old moral Catholic thing.

I wrote "Marriage" the same time I wrote "Bomb." That was a funny week. I did "Bomb" in about three or four days. I had a ball with it, because to get the shape, I had to type it down on paper first, and cut it out, each line, and paste it on big construction paper. So the glue was all sticky on my fingers, and then I said the heck with it, the publisher can always line it up.

ANDRE: As "Bomb" celebrates the atom bomb, "The Death of the Lucky Gent" seems to celebrate gang wars, street fights, knifing.

CORSO: Moralizing on things, this social shot could not be for me. I said "That's what it is and that's what's happening," and I let it jump.

ANDRE: You have a delight in that.

CORSO: I let it jump. Not a delight so much; I suffered under those Lucky Gents, you kidding? I was a kid, 13 years old in bad boys' homes, and there were about 15 blacks and one white kid, and they'd come in very hostile – this was in '43, when they had gangs in Harlem. Tiny Tims, they were the worst, these were the youngest ones. No, the Cubs were the youngest. The Tiny Tims were about 13, 15, 16, something like that.

There was no celebrating them at that time! But I can look at it very objectively. I realize when I got the shit beaten out of me, they had been fucked around.

ANDRE: In my interview with Robert Creeley a funny thing came up. We were talking about Richard Howard, and Bob said he thought Howard's essay[12] on you was very good. Do you?

CORSO: No, I don't know what he meant. I really know myself, and I thought, "Well, maybe somebody else can see something in me," because I met him maybe two or three times, so he gets his shot from what I write. Anybody is going to take me for what I write, then I have the trump card. After all, I know what I am putting down there and why I am putting it down. The poet and his poetry are inseparable.

ANDRE: Some things I thought were quite insightful. He seemed to predict that you would use the device of chance in organization.

CORSO: Yes, chance. Fine.

ANDRE: I think that was good. One thing he really took out of context, I think: the line "Thought is all I know of death" as an expression of anti-intellectualism.

CORSO: Well, he's crazy, man. Anti-intellectual?

ANDRE: Perhaps non-intellectual.

CORSO: Oh, "non" is better. Remember my whole basis of background, environment would be mainly on the streets, not in a prep school; the language that I speak, the argot that I speak, have that sound. There are not many intellectuals who go through that route.

ANDRE: You stopped writing poems about jazz. Are you still interested in jazz?

CORSO: It was just that particular period, the poems were stating the time, the people, the heads that I knew. Now for instance with rock and roll, I happen to meet lots of people in that field, but it's not much of a head shot with them. I mean Bob Dylan really doesn't know what to say except on his paper and to sing. It's a *silenzio* number all the way. The others talk like Einstein with something missing.

ANDRE: In your poem "After Reading 'In the Clearing,'" you said – I can't quote it exactly – Ginsberg is all I care to understand of the living. Is that still true?

CORSO: That's probably generalizing too much. Allen's work to me is the sharpest thing that's being said. I like the early Auden, the *Christmas Oratorio* and *In Praise of Limestone*. I really got to digging Pound. You say Creeley? Yes, some Creeley is really fantastic. But then I couldn't put everybody's name down.

ANDRE: You mentioned Shelley. Did you learn a lot from the Romantics?

CORSO: Yes. From romantics, yes. But German romantics, not English. That's when I got in to the whole megagalactic shot, and into thinking of infinity and what is finite. Hölderlin would say in his poem, "Oh my feet of mountains." He wouldn't say, "Oh my mountains are feet." He says, "My feet of mountains," and his head is up there.

ANDRE: There was your thing about mountains falling into valleys.

CORSO: What is that in?

ANDRE: "Sura," that girl's name that I didn't know.

CORSO: Right. That was my first girlfriend. Her name was Hope [Savage]. Allen met her in India. She was in the Himalayas a long time. She went there in 1958, and has been there ever since. She was the only chick around the time of that beat thing. A girl who wrote poetry when she was nine years old. Her father was Mayor of Camden, South Carolina, and of course they thought she was mad. That was around 1950. They gave her shock treatment. They destroyed this girl. When I met her she had had it, and she was 17, and very brilliant. She cried every night, and I'd say, "What is it?" And she said "I don't know what they took away, and therefore I feel I could never do anything perfect or complete." And she was a beautiful artist. She wanted her Rimbaud, she wore capes and boots in the streets of the South, and she ends up in there, that's a tragedy. Part of the whole thing in America is changing of the kids and the family who pay 50 dollars a day in these quiet places like Stowbridge[13] in Massachusetts, these loony farms for the rich – they just put them there and give them the shock treatment, and that's a terrible thing.

Hope, uh? That whole symbolic thing with the name, it's very funny. And very early in the game she said revolution is the solution. Very early in the game. Very early, man, in 1953. Boy oh boy.

ANDRE: How did she get the name Sura?

CORSO: She changed it. She didn't want to be called Hope. She would read nothing past Swinburne. Whatever they took away from her, she wanted nothing of the moderns, not even me, though she loved me. She loved me because I liked Shelley and she liked Shelley, so I used to call her my Shelley with a cunt. (*Laughs*)

Oh, there have been victims all right, lots of them. Those hippies, if they think they suddenly blossomed, boy a lot of them paid for it in the Fifties – a lot of them.

6:00 p.m.

CORSO: I wasn't stuck with the mother thing because I never saw her. I might have been like Allen and Jack were. Since I never saw her, that could have been a weight too, I guess, later on in life. But no. Very early in the game I started writing poems about the mother. It's in here. There are poems about the mother in here.

ANDRE: The Vestal Lady – is she ... ?

CORSO: She is a kind of mother who wants a child.

ANDRE: Yes, she is a virgin. There are poems there about the mother's feet, like "Sea Chanty."

CORSO: That's what Pisces is, the feet, an anatomical shot, you know. The head is Aries, the neck is Taurus. The Zodiac fits the whole body.

ANDRE: That's interesting.

CORSO: The Zodiac takes 24,000 years. There's 12 signs, 2,000 years a shot, right? The Aquarian Age is going to be 2,000, the last 2,000 was Piscean – Christ the fisher of men, right? Then the Arian Age, you got your lamp, and you also got your Caesar and your Alexander, the God of War? Right? Then before that you've got Taurus, the worship of the bull in Crete. Then Gemini was communication, hieroglyphs and cuneiform, and before that Cancer, which is flood, the moon with tides, the big floods in the Bible and *Gilgamesh*. It's fantastic. Christianity just closed this thing down. You see people today play with astrology out of the blue, but the Babylonians had a very intelligent shot on it.

ANDRE: Allen talked a bit about the Gnostic tradition. Rather than the Christian tradition, would you say you are in the Gnostic tradition?

CORSO: I don't know. The thing that makes sense to me is the "reflection." Sophia, the counterpart of Yahweh, the master worker, the female component, is wisdom, reflects wisdom and light at once, to see itself, light, you know, so it's reflective. Everything in that reflection then comes into being like Yahweh or the gods that be till today, all part of a reflection. They're not even real; they're just part of a reflection of Sophia. Made an awful lot of sense to me that all this would be literally reflected from something else.

The Gnostics had something going there all right. And they were always hoping for change. Another interesting people to check out is the Bogomils.

ANDRE: I don't know about them.

CORSO: When I was in Greece and Egypt there were many Albanians there; a lot of the Greeks are just Albanian colonies. And Albania was built by the Bogomils. The Bogomils lived in communes. They created their own language, architecture, statues; and they believed just in Jesus – they didn't believe in Mary. Of course they were wiped out, and a lot of them escaped and settled in the islands of Greece and in Albania.

ANDRE: That's what you want to get into next!

CORSO: I'd like to see about the communes in Christian times – if that was so. If you think of today, you want a little peace in your commune, and yet with people doing in each other, you are not very safe there. That's why in the Kerouac poem I say a man who has everything in his house, you see, and nothing outside, makes home a place to hang himself. Right? I wanted to take that track with the Bogomils and see how people can have little areas where they all know each other, little pockets where a communal community can really make it. Not too many people, no overpopulation, all the noise of cars would drive them bananas. Here was the communal number coming down very early in the game, and they were wiped out; they had no weapons, they didn't want any of that.

ANDRE: Is that like the farm you all have up in Cherry Valley [New York]? Would you say that's a commune?

CORSO: No that's a respite place. I go there to take a rest, and to be amongst the trees and the animals and the vegetables, and you are at peace with yourself and can do your work and get away from the city.

Also, I think in the future a lot of silence will be coming down, if people take the Eastern thing of not so much talking in their head. It would be a universal kind of language that would be very, very small in a way, because when you do speak, I could really feel that it's there in all the things that you say.

ANDRE: This question is going to make you mad. Some neutral critics, that is, critics who praised some things and criticized others, said there was a lack of self-criticism. You let poems be printed that were of no value.

CORSO: There are some that are not very good, yes, I know that, and a lot of times I see it later on. But the self-criticism that's important for me, as I say, would be during the poem itself. That doesn't bug me. I don't get mad. As for individual poems, when you look at it and say it's not very good, that's your opinion. I might like the poem.

ANDRE: I don't think people would criticize *Elegiac Feelings American* that way; it seems an evenly good book.

CORSO: It could be criticized. I think the Kerouac poem is too long, repetitious. Like I said, when I write fast it's got the musical quality. There's too much about the tree in there because I didn't rework it. That was really written out CHOO-CHOO-CHOO ... like that, in one night.

ANDRE: It has a strange beauty to it.

CORSO: All right. That was done in one night, and of course the feeling was there. Here, in "The American Way," I say, "I am almost nationalistic." That's not true feeling. I really didn't understand what that meant, and thought of the poet as the universal being. Being nationalistic about something is being geographical. "Pot" was a very early poem. That was done in 1957; it should have been dated. If anybody reads that now in the latest book ...

ANDRE: Written in 1957, it was a prophecy.

CORSO: That's what I am saying. And look, where it says they will not assassinate the president. That should have been dated. This one here, "Of One Month's Reading of English Newspapers," all these sex crimes with kids. The English have this weird sex thing.

ANDRE: They do.

CORSO: But what a thing to lay out! Some things it's best to keep to yourself, you know. All right, so that's where I think is a mistake. That would be a mistake.

"The Poor Bustard" was done very early. It was published at Harvard in 1956. They didn't have enough poems to publish, so they went through magazines.

"Eastside Incidents" is early.

ANDRE: Right, earlier than *Gasoline*.

CORSO: The "Friend" thing is reprinted. It was published before, but without these other parts of the triptych. I didn't do enough work on the "World."

Here again, in "America Politica Historia," I say, "I am nationalistic." As I think more and more about it, these are not the feelings that I had at the time. If you have feelings for America, that doesn't mean you are nationalistic. It sounds fascistic, or some shit.

ANDRE: Here's "Ode to England & Her Language." You used some of that for a strange interlude in *American Express* when Mr. D. visits England. Which did you write first, the poem or the novel?

CORSO: Both around the same time in 1960–61. That's why I say I now realize the thing is to keep the notebooks that I do in order. As the mind flows at the time, I would really be writing not a poem, but prose, and it would fall in there, too, because that's what's in the mind at the time. I think the best way to know a poet's head is to get the thing just like it is in the notebook.

ANDRE: That's what you did with the "Geometric Poem." Are you going to reproduce your notebooks like that?

CORSO: Not reproducing the notebook, because then it would be too hard to read. Reproducing it in print; I think that will be the best number.

ANDRE: Philip Whalen, in his most recent book remarks that the poem is so much his notebook that he would like to reproduce it.

CORSO: Well, the notebooks are there, and they'll all go to colleges. They've got some here.

ANDRE: Yes, I know the man who sorted them.

CORSO: What they have here is covered with cat's piss and shit. The cats kept going to the bathroom in that room where my papers were. That paste stuff stinks for a long time. (*Laughs*)

ANDRE: You know that Hinderov character in *American Express* reminded me of a character in another novel, the Professor in *The Secret Agent*,[14] and I was just wondering if you have ever read *The Secret Agent*.

CORSO: No. You know the girl who is his antagonist? That's Sura, that's what she was like.

ANDRE: Were other characters molded on people in life? This is terrible but I keep thinking that both Simon and Allen have long beards.

CORSO: Oh no, Allen wouldn't behave like that. Simon would be more like Peter [Orlovsky]. No, Allen is not depicted in that. Burroughs is Mr. D. This drawing looks like him. And look at this drawing of Carrol, the ghost of Carrol; it looks just like Kennedy only I drew it before he was shot.

ANDRE: Right.

CORSO: The characters in *American Express* play too much of the eye game, you know, staring at each other like that. Hitler was doing that all the time. When he had all the powerheads around him in this place up in Berchtesgaden, he would stare to see who could eyedown who first. Speer wrote about that.

ANDRE: You were the central character; you were the young man who built the rooms under the American Express office?

CORSO: Yes. The birth was similar.

ANDRE: That was the central fact of your life? I mean, being abandoned after birth?

CORSO: The trauma hits you, I've been told, and you can't get away from it, no way, if you are one year old and your mother leaves you. Especially because I had the double whammy. They gave me to a woman who I thought was my mother, and took me away from her, because she wanted to keep me, and they didn't want that because my father said eventually he'd take me back, which was ten years later. That's a double whammy there, and I had no realization of it. It was probably there in my head. I don't know.

Not all the characters are fully themselves, anyway. That's one thing about fantasies – you can change them around a lot. One part I kind of failed at is, when they went to the little children's house at night.

(*Corso starts adding and crossing out lines in* Elegiac Feelings American *in preparation for a reading later that night.*)

ANDRE: What poem are you revising now?

CORSO: It's number 9 of "Eleven Times a Poem." It's not a revision, it's already been done, but I took it out, and now I want it back.

> Parsley-mouthed Miss Christ
> legging her hurricane cunt
> across the sex-dark flats, and
> The moon-eyed night
> rays across the path of the gay fucketeer, and
> The marble storied gate sways in the wind
> like a breathing frieze
> And "sanctuary! sanctuary!" cries she
> And "pity! pity!" he

I had two different versions. I threw this in fast because I was getting the book together. I liked the "gay fucketeer" better than, you know, the "amputated rapist."

Let's get to some heavy nitty-gritties.

ANDRE: It's hard to decide what's heavy and nitty-gritty.

CORSO: What did you think about Brodsky's thing in the *New York Times*?[15] The poets blow their minds in the States because they are ignored, whereas in Russia if you write anything they'll fall on your head.

ANDRE: In terms of Berryman and Plath, that's interesting.

CORSO: I don't know if it's those. Were they ignored? And in what sense? What does he mean? He figures in the States no one listens to poets, which I think is far off base. They are read more than ever. Back in the Forties, poetry wasn't going at all. Yales Younger Series would sell 300 copies. Then after Ferlinghetti's and Ginsberg's books got going, and sold tens of thousands ...

ANDRE: How do your books sell?

CORSO: Well, I only know by their printings. Some have had ten printings, some one. But I don't know how many copies Laughlin[16] comes out with a printing. I think 10,000 maybe. Ferlinghetti or Ginsberg, their things go into like 100,000. Mine not that much, but they keep on going, every year I get from these three books maybe two thou, something like that.

ANDRE: Have you ever thought of embodying some of that early trauma directly in your poetry?

CORSO: Well, as I say, it comes out in *Vestal Lady* in those mother poems. I don't know the trauma; I was told that it was, but I don't know it. The earliest memory I have is with the second woman, and that was a real nice one. I was in a bathtub with her, when I was three years old, and I saw the black hair on the mound on the cunt and the water, and to me that was a good shot to remember, because you have the contemporary poem of birth with that old water thing, right?

ANDRE: That's nice. You could have written confessional poems?

CORSO: I don't remember any horror show of "Mama, Mama, where are you?" What's to confess?

ANDRE: If you'd chosen I suppose you could have emphasized the negative and unhappy elements, but you've never done that? Have you? I don't think so.

CORSO: I think they come up. All right, they say, the child is a genius. But what about the one who lugs his childhood about? That's not genius; it's lugging a thing back from the past. But if you've got that in yourself, the child in yourself, that's okay.

I always had this clash with the two. I have very much of the child in me, and I had the thought of that child who grew up. But when it's like carrying the weight of the child, I knew how to lessen the load.

That's why dreams are so great. Dreams helped me out an awful lot. I remember I was 16 years old when I dreamed that I saw myself dead on a highway, and I said, "What am I doing lying there like that, neglected?" So I picked myself up, uh? and carried myself. And away in the distance I see there is a mortuary, and I say, "I'll bring it in there and see what they are going to do." Then I say, "No, I take the body back." So I keep on walking and it just falls into dust. I never realized who was carrying this dead weight. It was a good little dream.

I realize now of all the things I've gone through and seen, and the good heads that I've met, and all the nonsense and all the essence, you throw away the nonessential and keep the essence, the goodies. And nothing should any more be confessional or laid down like that, but really objective and dig the shot outside of me, and how it affects me, and then set it down. That to me would be truth, whereas the confessional doesn't come close to truth. It's not a universal truth, it's a personal truth, something that needs to be laid out like that.

ANDRE: Also, confessional implies some sort of guilt.

CORSO: Yes, the ego guilt, too. That's one thing that I don't have. Nothing about that shot of the past, unless I were to believe in karma. Nay, nay.

ANDRE: Nay, Nay. You use archaism well in your poetry.

CORSO: Yes, I would use a word like "thee" but I'd make sure I use "you" in it too, you know.

ANDRE: There is a silly article, accusing that of being academic.

CORSO: Thee?

ANDRE: I thought it was silly.

CORSO: I just like the sounds of those words, man. Good God, using thou – academic! What is academic anyway?

ANDRE: It refers to the color grey.

CORSO: I use it in "Bomb" but only because it has something apocalyptical and biblical, like "ye BANG ye BONG ye BING." There's a lot of interplay in that poem. When it's read, it's a sound poem.

If one checks out my poems, you could really think, wow, did this guy want that big holocaust, this monstrosity, was he nationalistic? Like Ferlinghetti got screwed up about "Power." "It's fascistic," and I said, "No, that word should be taken from that particular area. It's a great poetic word, and I want to see what I can do," and I played all different numbers in that "Power."

ANDRE: In reading it, I became aware that the word was a neutral word. It was defined by the adjective – imaginative power, cruel power.

CORSO: Everything came after that – gay power, black power, flower power.

ANDRE: In the ninth part of "Eleven Times a Poem" you say, "It were far better to demonstrate for peace / than sue for it." Are you detached from the whole war thing?

CORSO: Yes, completely. How do I look at wars?

> War
> is to deplore
> when peace generates hate
> between the infernal patriot
> and those who demonstrate

You know, the hardhats going downtown and beating up on people.

> Yet war is hard to deplore
> a great part of life for man throughout history
> has been the times of war – O how real and hard a thing!

The whole thing in Vietnam has just lost all meaning, legendariness. Whereas the Vietnamese, no matter how much they are being bombed they've got something to go for.

I just wonder, unless they are being attacked, if they can ever again get anybody here to get up and go.

ANDRE: The last poem in that sequence struck me as Audenesque.

CORSO: No. That's funny. Why?

ANDRE: Auden would tend to personify things that way, the Trickster with the capital T.

CORSO: This is the Indians going to school. There's Young Man Afraid of His Horses in the classroom. It's all the Indian chiefs, Crazy Horse and Little Wolf, going to this school like you see in books with a lady with big boobs trying to teach them. I put them all together, like I did in "Botticelli's 'Spring.'" I put Dante with Michelangelo in a particular period, right? So I put all those in a classroom.

ANDRE: I see. Auden's not relevant. You're right.

CORSO: One is bound to hit sound of others. "You, Whose Mother's Lover Was Grass," you said, was Dylan Thomasy.

ANDRE: Who is "The Senile Genius?"

CORSO: No one in particular.

ANDRE: I thought you were referring to someone specific, one of our older great poets, perhaps?

CORSO: No. It's a sad thing about genius when it does get that way, because you'd think the next step would be divine. You have talent, then you have genius, then you have divine. That's how I see it – three stages. I call Dante divine; I don't say genius.

ANDRE: Well, what would senile genius be?

CORSO: It means they just stopped there, you see? (*Laughs*)

ANDRE: That's interesting.

CORSO: Some were truncated with their talent, some were truncated with their genius. Right? We talk about the child and the genius; then we have the senile genius, one who has fully matured, bloomed, blossomed, but nonetheless did not take the other step.

A lot of people say, "Wow, he's talented." Then it's "What do you do with your talent?" Then you have "Wow, that's real genius." And then in your next step you really put that genius into something really fantastic. And again I think I would use some of Shelley's poetry and Dante. I think I was writing about *all* the geniuses who …

ANDRE: … stopped. Far out.

CORSO: And again divine doesn't have to hit any kind of spiritual or theological shot – vision, you know.

ANDRE: Earlier in "Eleven Times a Poem" you call Socrates the "wisest man of earth." Why?

CORSO: I don't know now. He was a very, very smart fucker all right, but now I realize he didn't understand poets. He'd just see them drunk in bars, you know. When he was dying he said, "All I know is I know nothing." I didn't like that. It cuts it off – a good way.

Well, who was wiser than Socrates? All you've got today is just teachers of philosophy. You don't have any philosophers today. The poets are the ones who open their mouths today; the philosophers I don't hear. Whereas in Socrates' time, the poets weren't saying anything, but the philosophers were. And he died very Christ-like; he did the wise move. Shelley put Socrates, Buddha and Christ behind the chariot in "The Triumph of Life." You know why? Because they didn't write anything.

Now look at a man like Buddha. He's a little earlier than Socrates. Well, he has to sit 40 years under a tree to check out his shot. Look how long that took him, to find something very simple. Maybe it wasn't then. To find out what death meant, what it was, then after 40 years, he said, "Ah, I know, life is the cause of death." A very simple number. Like the wheel, uh?

Before Socrates or Buddha, who was there that they could get the flame from? They didn't have anybody.

ANDRE: Thinking of your two Indian poems …

CORSO: There is one called "Death of the American Indian God,"[17] right?

ANDRE: The other[18] uses the concluding lines from that.

CORSO: They were the redmen
                    feathers-in-their-head men
                    now
                    down among the dead men
                    how

ANDRE: (*Laughs*) In many ways there is as much left to study in the American Indian civilization as in Greek civilization.

CORSO: Oh, not in architecture, anyway, except the pueblo. I would think the Indians had a better way of life, but …

The Greeks could have had technology. The Renaissance picked up on that, through the Byzantine; Giotto learned the two dimensional Christ from the Byzantine.

ANDRE: You have many poems coming out of paintings, like "Saint Francis" was composed to the series by Giotto. Did someone suggest that to you, like Browning or Williams?

CORSO: No. I just *love* paintings. I just flitted about all the museums of Europe; I was in love, looking at the Uccellos and the Masaccios. And then it would just hit me as a subject.

That and zoos. It was not like being in a tower. It was going out observing. What was the prettiest thing that I could observe? Animals, but in the sad state of a zoo, or great works of art.

ANDRE: The poem on the mandrill in *Vestal Lady* – did that come from a zoo?

CORSO: Yes. You know what that poem is called? "Vision Epizootics." Epizootic means pertaining to the zoo. Now what kind of vision was that? I go to the zoo and see a mandrill. Then the mandrill is in my head, right? So I can easily project it out – that's the vision – and write about it. So what do I see now? Not the one in the zoo, but the one sitting at the foot of my bed, doing just what he was doing in the zoo – eating mice. (*Laughs heartily*)

Well, I could call that a vision.

ANDRE: That's a different use of the word.

CORSO: I use a "vision agent" – things like that. I have a vision agent in my poetry. Twice I used vision agents.

ANDRE: Who is the vision agent?

CORSO: The vision agent comes out when I go to Rotterdam; then he comes out when I am in Cambridge, and takes me through the underground. Okay? That means someone who is sending me off somewhere to see something. I used that to go to Rotterdam and see – what do I see? – to Rotterdam in World War II. I heard it was bombed a lot, right? And I see it now.

ANDRE: I can't think of another poem where you bring animals back from the zoo. Is there another one you can name?

CORSO: There is the puma in the Chapultepec Zoo, the American cow in the Mexican zoo, the tamarinds who seek phalangers to flay …

ANDRE: What is that phalanger in "Mutation of the Spirit?"

CORSO: It's a little animal.

ANDRE: What's the great blond-fuzz moth earlier in the poem? Have you seen them?

CORSO: No. It's a moth I made big. That's what the Visigoths looked like to me – blond beard and hair, but wild, right? Barbarous, right?

ANDRE: Was there some specific book behind "The Death of the American God?"

CORSO: A lot of Indians I met in California didn't dig that.

ANDRE: It seems to me that there are certain inaccuracies in it.

CORSO: The Mandans were wiped out, they wore blankets, they played lacrosse on the ice, the women did press tapioca, they wore weasel tufts.

ANDRE: Well, I may be wrong, but I thought the caribou was an arctic animal.

CORSO: It's cold, there was snow. I figured the caribou would be around. But that might not be the fact. You might be right. The Pawnees were up towards South Dakota.

ANDRE: "Spontaneous Requiem for the American Indian," the other Indian poem, mentions Kiwago, Wakonda and Talako. Who were they?

CORSO: Kiwago is the big bull buffalo. The white buffalo is Kiwago. Wakonda is the great sky god, but also earth god. Wakonda takes in the whole shot, whereas Talako is the sky god. Talako would be like Horus in ancient Egypt, Hermes in Greece. Wakonda is more the great spirit. I was a counselor at a boys' camp called Camp Kiwago.

ANDRE: No guff?

CORSO: I put on some little plays for them about a coyote man that brought fire, who made human beings, who was the Prometheus of the Indians. And through it I checked out the other gods.

ANDRE: What's "deatheme" in that poem?

CORSO: Oh that's just a created word – death theme. (*Picks up Andre's copy of* Long Live Man *open at "First Night on the Acropolis" and reads.*) "Usual cheap commonplace rhymes!" What!?

ANDRE: Well, I uh.

CORSO: That's the nicest last line I got.

ANDRE: I didn't expect …

CORSO: (*The last lines of the poem* –) "I cried for my shadow that dear faithful sentry / splashed across the world's loveliest floor."

ANDRE: Do you ever think you use easy rhymes?

CORSO: This is too easy, you're right. But, what the Hell, if I use some hard ones, why can't I use the easy ones?

One of the publisher's friends, Hayden Carruth, got me to change a rhyme in "Sura." It made better sense before.

> Twist the elf's knotty arm it must drawl thuds of joy.
> Light must return
> And reprieve the earth with its merciful stain.
> – Fairy, tip the urn.

Originally I had "Twist the elf's knotty arm it must drawl thuds of pain." I don't see why it shouldn't be "pain," but I'd rather have joy anyway. (*Laughs heartily*)

ANDRE: "Sura" is a terrific poem:

> Hurry! Mountains are falling on valleys.
> Trees are getting lost.

What about other poets? What about Frank O'Hara? He was as lively a poet as you.

CORSO: Frank had fire all right, and very metropolitan. I liked that about him. When he mentions his friends' names, he is not name-dropping. In other words, people he was associated with, that was his life, and he incorporated them into his work. Whereas many of the other poets would write poems to each other and mention their names in there, and it was like writing a poem called "Poetry," and putting Poetry in the poem, and I thought that was just a little too much. But Frankie got away with it nicely because it was his milieu; they were all New York City people, the artists, the abstract expressionists, and he was working at the Museum and what not ...

The only thing I looked for, and I think I found it, was profundity. It might be just too light, you know? How deep can this man get? And lots of times I realized that though it sounded light, it was very, very profound. Oh, I liked Frank an awful lot. I remember the first time I heard something from Frank O'Hara was in 1954 at Harvard – a poem about a tiger leaping over the table and pissing in the flower pot as he leapt over. I thought that was great, just that one line.

Other poets? I like some of Michaux. Some of the Russians – Andrei Voznesensky. The other one I don't know about.

ANDRE: Yevtushenko?

CORSO: I don't get too much feeling out of it. Smart, you know? Smart. Did you see that Madison Square thing?

ANDRE: That's just what I was going to ask.

CORSO: Doubleday sent me tickets – a nice ticket right at the front.

ANDRE: Those singers in the background, man …

CORSO: That's what performance is; sometimes it comes out like that. I just sat back and looked. I can get just as much from looking at a man's books and tell if I like it or not. Sometimes I get up there and stammer away, drunk or something. So I can't very well judge him for that and say that's what he is. No, I don't get much from him, but I do from Voznesensky.
    I like Randall Jarrell. Some of his things are very sharp.
    Now, who else is there? A lot of people. Kerouac's poetry, yes, because he would hit it like I would hit it. He would just write them out fast, but with no change.

ANDRE: You and Allen and Kerouac all seem to write like that.

CORSO: Not … Allen makes sure he gets that form in there. I rework, but only at the time of writing. I don't think I could let things go out without change. Only when I call a poem "spontaneous." Naturally, all my poems are spontaneous, literally, but in particular ones there are no changes; they just zap out like that. You need a particular rhythm to have them that way. In "Spontaneous Requiem for the American Indian" I could see the form coming in, knowing when I got stuck I could always go to the repetition of old requiems.

ANDRE: Have you been interested in Eastern religions at all?

CORSO: I don't think I am interested in any religion. I mean, I like to know all I can of all the religions, but not as a thing to fall into. I don't think that's possible. I dig that, having the information all worked out in my head, so that I could have unity of being somehow, rather than getting hung on just one thing.
    I have to see the East. I want to do that. Most people I know who go to

India come back very different. They come back Indiophiles or something.

ANDRE: John Giorno I think was the last one.

CORSO: Yes, he and a lot of people. Allen picked up good things for the reason that he went there with something. When you go with something you can come back with something in addition. Lots of people I know who went without anything came back "instant swamis," and I knew they'd sucked them in.

HUMOR, THE BUTCHER:
AN INTERVIEW WITH GREGORY CORSO
Victor Bockris

We ran into Gregory Corso and friends outside St. Mark's Church one night. Gregory had been inside, selling self-portraits to the audience, and now he wanted to smoke and eat, so we hailed a cab and headed off for the Hotel Chelsea. It was starting to rain. We reached the Chelsea, warmed up with a bottle of wine and a joint, and sat across from a grinning Mr. G. to begin ...

CORSO 1973

BOCKRIS: Signor Corso, what do you know?

CORSO: I know all there is to know, because there ain't that much to know.

BOCKRIS: What's the worst thing that could happen to you?

CORSO: I could kill someone.

BOCKRIS: What's the best thing that could happen to you?

CORSO: That everyone would love me.

BOCKRIS: What do you consider the strongest trait of your personality?

CORSO: I don't have no personality.

BOCKRIS: What's humor?

CORSO: Gregory Nunzio Corso. "Humor" is one of those biggie words, like "Love," "God," "Truth." For me, it's a terrible butcher at times; it gets rid of the shit.

BOCKRIS: Are you happy?

CORSO: Oh yes! Yes! Never have I been so happy as I have in the past month and a half. Because I learned how to be nice.

BOCKRIS: How did you learn to be nice?

CORSO: From one day taking for granted my friends, those who love me and those who didn't. I don't walk around like a wide-eyed jerk. No one can hurt me. Even if a guy came up with a pistol and went "pow pow," I wouldn't be hurt.

BOCKRIS: Are there any mysteries?

CORSO: Generally, no. Personally, one.

BOCKRIS: What's the one?

CORSO: I don't know who I am.

THE FIRST POEM

BOCKRIS: Do you remember when you wrote your first poem?

CORSO: Yes. I remember it well.

BOCKRIS: When was it?

CORSO: 1946. I was 16 years old, standing on a subway. It wasn't too crowded. I asked myself about the people, and by asking myself that, I got faint, got scared. I got off at the wrong stop. I went to a movie. It's a dreadful magnificence, to look and see. It took me 16 years – not bad! I was in a good prepared, smart poet state, to write my first poem. The subject was my mother, whom I'd never seen, about whom I was lied to all the time, that she'd gone away, she was a whore … I spouted it on the rooftop of the Educational Alliance on East Broadway, thereon wobbling a sea chanty!

BOCKRIS: Song?

CORSO: Yes. "My mother hates the sea …" It's in my first book, *The Vestal Lady on Brattle.*

POETRY IS A GOODIE

BOCKRIS: Why is poetry so unpopular?

CORSO: I never thought that. Life is beautiful; it's people who mess it up. Poetry is beautiful; it's poets who mess it up. There's nothing wrong with life, and nothing wrong with poetry.

BOCKRIS: Do you think poetry could get more popular, like rock, so poets could earn more money?

CORSO: No. No way. We're talking about a high-class expression of human history. It goes and goes, and it's the poet that makes it go. It's the poet itself, that's it. It's such a goodie. Like marijuana is a goodie. Poetry's there. It can't be decimated by a lack of audience.

BOCKRIS: You're about to bring out a new book?[1]

CORSO: Yeah. It'll take about a year. Title? I don't know. But it's the first time I sat at the desk and felt like a wise old fucker.

GREGORY'S PROPHECIES

I lay forth some of my prophecies:

1. In the "Marriage" poem, grab the mayor and tell him, "When are you gonna stop killing whales?" In America, they stopped killing whales.

2. In 1959, in the last line of a poem,[2] I said, "Richard Nixon will be the last president." 'Cause they're not going to look up to one man anymore. That doesn't mean the fall of America or nothing; my prophecies don't

hurt anyone. My prophecies have never been religious; I took prophecy out of religion. My prophecies were almost like commands. The Beats were like commanders: "Let this be!" and so it was. That's the closest thing to braggadocio I'll ever get!

3. *Newsweek,* 1963: I said, "The kids are so much sharper, so much smarter these days." And I was right. I know it's gonna be better. Not out of desperation, but it could be the way you want it to be. And that's as far as we can go with life.

THE BEAT MOSES

I have my finger on the decal number. The Fifties ignited something of a mental evolve. It was the Fifties that did it, like an Ice Age, a crack in consciousness. The beatniks, the literary ones, were like Moses taking the slaves out of Egypt. There's one fantastic little fuckup that's going on. You'll never know when you go. The weight of death is never with the dead; it's with the living.

THE GOLDEN CALF

The Sixties was The Golden Calf. Beautiful Bob Dylan, the Jefferson Airplane … but it was still The Golden Calf – that meant obeyance. They were stuck. They wanted their message through The Golden Calf – music. I stayed out. They're gonna have to move on, to The Promised Land.

WEATHERVANE

The Seventies is a respite. They're gonna check out their sources and know who they are. I'm a weathervane; I go, so shall ye go! And the best way to do it would be, if they encounter me, they better be nice to me. And if they don't encounter me, they better be nice to whoever they encounter.

You can't miss out with humor and truth. All the rest sucks.

I'M POOR SIMPLE HUMAN BONES: AN INTERVIEW WITH GREGORY CORSO
Robert King

Gregory Corso, with Lawrence Ferlinghetti, Allen Ginsberg, Michael McClure, Shig Murao, Peter Orlovsky, Miriam Patchen, Kenneth Rexroth and Gary Snyder, spent the blizzardy week of March 18, 1974, in Grand Forks, North Dakota, participants in the Fifth Annual University of North Dakota Writers Conference: City Lights in North Dakota. "Conference," in retrospect, does not seem the most appropriate noun to describe what actually happened; it was a weeklong festive reunion of the Beats: poetry readings, long open microphone rap sessions with large audiences, mantras, a large exhibit of Kenneth Patchen's art. Unlike a Ginsberg reading at Jersey City State College not too long ago where, according to Jane Kramer, the teacher introducing Ginsberg snatched back the microphone to proclaim, "This evening does not receive the endorsement of the English Department," the City Lights "Conference" was sponsored by the UND English Department. Various members of the Department interviewed each of the poets, often under less than ideal circumstances. So crowded was the week with activities, so responsive and enthusiastic the largely student audiences.

The interview that follows took place at Robert King's home the afternoon of March 22, 1974. John Little, who heads the committee responsible for the Conference, also participated in the conversation, as did Doug Rankin, a UND student.

James McKenzie

KING: In the introduction to *Gasoline* you said in your seventeenth year that people handed you books of illumination out of adjoining cells. Did that really happen? What were they?

CORSO: They were really dumb-ass books to begin with. There was Louis Beretti, first of all. Henderson Clarke wrote all these books about Little Italy, gangster books. That was what convicts read. All right. Now the smart man was the man who handed me *Les Miserables*. And you know who did that? Me. When I went to the prison library, I looked at that fat book and I knew what miserable meant. I was 16 and a half. When I said they passed me books of illumination, I meant they handed me something else, not the books. Yeah, there was a guy who had a beautiful standard dictionary. He loved me, man. And he had this old standard dictionary and I studied every fucking word in that book. 1905. This big, it was. All the archaic, all the obsolete words. That's illumination, I guess.

KING: Okay, okay. Following that up, there's a lot of talk now about primitive poets as models. And now we've got Rothenberg putting out anthologies, and this kind of thing. So you must have been into that early?

CORSO: No. No, but I think I am called an original and also very much a primitive type, too, in poetry. How it came to me, though, was high class. You see. Wow. I mean the first feeling I had when I wrote my first poem was like music coming through a crack in the wall, and I felt good writing it.

KING: So you're not consciously trying to recapture primitive forms or feelings?

CORSO: I'll tell you, I know the sestina, I know the sonnets, I know the old sources of the information that I lay out. Go back to your sources, I tell people, but not as much as my friends do about the earth, or growing food, but the head. I say check yourself out, how far back you can go that way to your sources. And this I might have gotten from the Tibetans, because they say if you're conscious on your death bed, try to think back to your mother's cunt because you came in as you go out. It's good exercise for poets. I had to go back through history to get back as far as I could go to the sources, cave paintings as I say, and all that.

KING: You talk a lot about *Gilgamesh, The Book of the Dead,* these kinds of things.

CORSO: Right. That's all relay. It passes memory. See, if you forget the past, it's gone. And who was it, Santayana who said if you don't understand your mistakes you're going to have to repeat them. A karma shot, right? I don't think anything was a mistake. I'll hold to *Gilgamesh,* I'll hold to the Bible, I'll hold to all those goodies. They're all relays.

KING: Did you ever think about going to the university and majoring in comparative literature?

CORSO: Well, I went to Harvard, now. It was funny, on the banks of the Charles, drinking beer, talking about Hegel, Kierkegaard, it was nice – MacLeish's class. He'd sit there like the White Father, you know, people laughing, reading their poems, criticizing each other. I just went to one because he invited me up there, and immediately I saw Keats's death mask on the wall, and immediately I said, "Ah, that's Keats." Burroughs is beautiful, teaching at CCNY. He's really got the kids going: Do you sincerely want to be a writer; that's what he's teaching. The word "sincere" is too much. As long as human beings sing, it's beautiful. In other words, man, if they want to let themselves go, that's beautiful. And they don't know what a nice teacher they have in Burroughs. What a shot that is. And that's what works.

KING: What about poets you read early, early influences?

CORSO: The one who really turned me on very much was Shelley, not too much his poetry, but his life. I said, "Ah, a poet then could really live a good life on this planet." That fucker was beautiful, a sharp man. But dumb in a way. He went to free Ireland. You know how he did it? In a rowboat, halfway sinking in a rowboat.

KING: More his life than his poetry?

CORSO: The poet and poetry are inseparable. You got to dig the poet. Otherwise the poetry sucks. If I dug the poet, then automatically the poetry worked for me. Edgar Allen Poe the same way. Then there are some poets, I just don't buy their books, I don't dig it. Pound makes it, Auden made it for me. I mean, Auden is good. I dig Auden, you see. A lot don't. Listen, Allen wanted to sing mantras to him, and Auden said, "No, I get embarrassed by somebody singing to me. I don't want it." So Allen said, "That dumb fuck, he died and didn't realize who I was, man. I was singing to him."

KING: Auden's life doesn't seem particularly exciting; he's certainly no Shelley.

CORSO: Naw, he didn't dig Shelley, but he did dig *The Tempest*. That's Shakespeare's best shot. That's the time of the "dopey fuck" remark. Auden was reading *The Tempest* to me and it sounded beautiful. I was just a kid. Walking down the street, afterwards, feeling good, I was crossing the street when this fucking taxi driver says, "Get out of the way, you dopey fuck." Here I am alive with poetry, right? I go home, look in the mirror: am I a dopey fuck? No way!

KING: You talk about a new consciousness in *Elegiac Feelings American*. What do you mean by that, or what do you see as a new consciousness?

CORSO: That's what's happening, and very fast. It took a while for this body to make it, but the head's going beautiful. Now I took the daddies and I said that truth was the Seventies hit. But truth is the pole vault that stops you. You say, "Well, I believe in this" and then you stop with it. So it's almost as bad as the word "faith" because people believe in things they don't understand by their faith. I'd rather have a little bit of knowledge than a whole lot of faith. So humor then comes after it. Humor is the butcher that gets rid of the shit. I love Americans for that, man; if they can laugh at something, it's finished.

KING: Does America, as a country, spiritual entity, whatever, ask something different from its poets than other countries ask? There's Whitman, and then there's Crane, maybe there's the Fifties ... but I don't see guys wandering around worried about being a French poet.

CORSO: Do you know how Hart Crane got fucked up? Hart Crane took the two great American poets, Edgar Allen Poe and Walt Whitman. Now, Edgar Allen Poe is in, Whitman is out. So poor Hart Crane was like an accordion, in and out, in and out. He didn't last too long, but he knew his shot. He knew who his two daddies were.

KING: Do you feel some kind of stress to express America?

CORSO: Oh yeah, I love America, I love America. And I know why. You take a mystical number, say like Columbus coming over in the Santa Maria. That may be the second coming, but it'd be the geographical number rather than a baby being born out there.

KING: You say you love America and you do, but you're ambivalent about it, like you're afraid to go into an American Express office or, in a poem,[1] you're afraid to go into an American Express office.

CORSO: It was a drag all the time, man, I love them but I had to wait in line for the mail, first of all, right. And you've got these old ladies from Duluth going "Ugh" to me. It was a drag going to the American Express.

KING: But you mean more than that. I mean you're not really talking about some hassle with the American Express. You're talking about some other America, or maybe the existing America.

CORSO: I'm talking about the America whose applecart I upset, man. It's gone. The old cornball America, you know, where people are all regimented and all that shit. I mean, look at you with your hair and all that.

KING: And in that Kerouac poem,[2] you talk a lot about the fact that there are two Americas. He keeps looking for one and there's one there but that's not the one he was looking for.

CORSO: Right. It was never there, you see. Whitman was at a time that was virginal and now we've got the birth.

KING: There's a feeling around, some of it unjustified, and some of it comes out of your comments and other people's comments, that books are a drag, and even the past is a drag, and everything should be spontaneous, that therefore there's no craft in your poetry. What would you say about the craft of poetry as you practice it?

CORSO: As I practice it, I say I build a brick musehouse. The craft is there, man. See, words have only been written down in the last 400 years. It was always sung before that. And it's gotten back to the cycle where it's sung again with Dylan. Okay. Now. But I still say "You can just sit there, Gregory, and make the music on the page, too. Don't get up there and twang away." I use the expression "brightness falls from the air. Many a queen has died young and fair."[3] That's beautiful music.

LITTLE: Do you have a built in sense of form?

CORSO: Yeah, I know I do. Oh sure. The "bing bang bong boom" hit it, right, with the "Bomb" poem. I mean that was real music coming out on its own, and I don't have to knock myself out too fast with it, you know.

KING: But you don't worry around about syllables or stress or …?

CORSO: I like to rhyme when I want to rhyme. When I don't want to rhyme I don't rhyme. It's all music.

LITTLE: How did you get that sense of form? You never did cultivate it, never did study the sonnet?

CORSO: That's the whole shot; if I did I wouldn't have had it. I know the sonnet … I can do the sonnet, the sestina.

LITTLE: It was there.

CORSO: Yeah, because it's obvious to be there, it's one of the simplest things. Just do what you want to do, right? And poetry, top shot poesy. I mean, that's the top profession, man. I walk down the street in New York, you know, I feel great sometimes. I look at those fuckers making millions with their Cadillacs and their businesses. But you, Corso, your fucking profession's beautiful.

KING: Do you live in New York most of the time now?

CORSO: Yeah, that's the city I'm most comfortable in.

KING: Do you run into New York poets? By that I mean, you know, the people who call themselves the New York poets.

CORSO: I don't meet many people. I used to know Frank O'Hara. Now he was good. Now don't bother much; sometimes I go to OTB and play the horses.

KING: Do you think your poetry has changed since 1955?

CORSO: You can see that's a progression there. The next book I know is going to be a top shot for me. Yeah, real smart little numbers. Those were all like just exploding out of me. This time I'm going to really look at them and say, "Okay, Corso." If I was building cars or was a carpenter I would talk that way – I'd say I built something nice – so I'll do it with poetry.

KING: You seem to me sometimes to have two basic kinds of things that you do, which is not to suggest limits but identify a couple of things. One is a real conversational kind of thing: "32nd Birthday," for example; the other verges on incantation, "Requiem for the Indian," "Coit Tower," "Spontaneous Requiem for the American Indian." Do you try to write any one kind of poetry now?

CORSO: I don't want to write elegies anymore. I don't want to get stuck, I don't want to write elegies for people, you know. And so I think that's done. Going to museums and zoos, I wrote a lot about. I felt for the animals in the zoo, and I felt the learning from seeing the great paintings, and all that. Now a very different shot in my poetry, very different number. I'd rather now live the life than writing it out on the page. But when it does come out, very rare now, seldom, it grows, like I say, a brick musehouse.

KING: You think you're writing less now than you were?

CORSO: I'm writing songs, now; I always have written songs; and to me they're love poems. People say there aren't very many love poems written today, right? I don't have to call my poems love poems, but they *are* love poems. I'm going to call these songs, though, this next book; that's the shot, man, so that the *word* has still got the music in it rather than twanging with the guitar up there, right?

KING: Do you do more readings now than you did?

CORSO: No. I haven't read for a long time.

KING: Do you have a small circle of friends in New York, or a wide circle of friends, or are you a loner?

CORSO: Yeah, I guess more of a loner than anything else. See, when I took drugs, that eliminated a lot of friends because you're always hitting them up for money and all that. They don't like that. So it's good; I got rid of them. Mainly, I sleep with my cats and the female. I love female. I've been with this one female now for a year. I like living with female. I keep close to her and all that; I don't bother much with the outside.

KING: In *Elegiac Feelings*, "Geometric Poem" is an interesting thing. It's handwritten, it's got little drawings on it.

CORSO: Yeah, but it's wrong. You see, the Italian edition[4] was great because it's big. That's when I learned Egyptian. But the way New Directions did it, it's very small, you need a magnifying glass. New Directions books are a particular size. So I said to him, "Don't publish the poem, I think that would just screw it up; just leave that one out." But then I realized, if you're talking about elegiac feelings, American, Gregory, and you want to go back to your sources, and the Egyptians are undoubtedly the sources, with the elegies, right? With the death shot.

KING: Do you have a good relationship with New Directions?

CORSO: Yeah.

KING: Why did you leave Ferlinghetti?

CORSO: Oh, I didn't leave Ferlinghetti. Ferlinghetti left me. You see, I wrote a poem called "Power" – that's in my *Happy Birthday of Death*. My "Marriage" is in there, and some of the real goodies in that book. But Ferlinghetti thought it was fascistic; he didn't understand I was changing the word "power." I said, "Why can't a poet handle this word, break the meaning of it?" So he wouldn't publish it. Now, I got very insulted that he sent it to some San Francisco publisher who also refused. So I said, "Well, bullshit, give me my book back," and wrote to New Directions and said, "Hey, you who publish Pound and Rimbaud, do you like long poems?" because these were long single word poems: "Army," "Power," "Police," "Marriage," – and Laughlin wrote back, "Of course," and took the book. And Larry, years later then suddenly realized, and said, "Gregory, yeah." This is a straight story, it's not downing Larry. I got to dig Larry very well, man, on this trip. I guess the one guy I didn't get too close to was Snyder, you know, because he left too soon; I don't know him too well. I dig the man a lot. I wasn't trying to sabotage anything; I think that Allen thought that I was trying to sabotage his feeling about how to survive on this planet, right? And I could get no way edgewise to say it's also a mental evolve though, too, folks, also the head – take care of it.

LITTLE: Has your relationship changed much with Snyder?

CORSO: I don't know him that well. I knew that man very early in the game, but as I say not that well.

LITTLE: Has it changed with the other poets here?

CORSO: Well, it's gotten nice with Ferlinghetti, and Allen's my old friend. He lives in New York; I see him all the time.

LITTLE: They seem to be putting up with you at times.

CORSO: I don't think Ferlinghetti though. Larry was mostly the one who did not admonish me.

LITTLE: Gregory, you said earlier that the Beats have hurt themselves but they never hurt anybody else. Gary Snyder says a different sort of thing. He said that the Beats were aware that they had to take some responsibility for the kind of things that had happened to people who had misused drugs. I was wondering if they don't have some of the same concern for you.

CORSO: Allen has a tendency, and he might be right – a tendency to care too much for me, to come on like a daddy, you know, and tell me, "Well, Gregory, take care of yourself" and all this bit. And I had to finally straighten him out and say, "Look, Allen, we're peers, man. And if I live my way – you sit and meditate, that's good. I'm not telling you that I dig it, but you do. But I live my way." It's the only way, man, otherwise, you know, we'd break intercourse.

LITTLE: So you don't think that they feel protective toward you, that they see in you a projection of things that they once recommended that maybe they no longer do?

CORSO: I think they really want to do sincerely good; I think they're telling people right and maybe some way in life how to take care of yourself. I think that's good, but that's not my hit. Mine is the mental shot; I say, "Great, if you know the info, if you've got the knowledge, get your sources ... I love it.

Whether you drink, or smoke or what your farm is like and all that, I'm not interested."

KING: Do you make a living off poetry?

CORSO: No.

KING: How do you live?

CORSO: Oh, maybe that I do because I can sell my manuscripts, and I get good money for them. Also readings; and so sporadically I do make monies. I never had to steal or anything when I used to buy dope, for instance. I never had to steal for it. But they're books, notebooks, that I write in.

LITTLE: Who do you sell them to and how much do they pay you?

CORSO: Oh, I give them to Gotham Book Mart in New York, which sells them to Columbia or to the University of Texas at Austin. They get half the monies and I get a half, rather than me dealing direct with these universities. I get what, about $200 a book when I need money. It's terrible, years ago the poor poets, man, they did nothing. They'd just throw them away or lose them or some shit, right? When I needed money for dope, you see, I would never recopy out the poems. I'd just sell the book. So a lot of my poems, you know, are in the universities and have never been published … from 1965 to now. But the goodies I remember in my head. *Elegiac Feelings* came out only because of the death of Kerouac. The other poems, the elegies on Kennedy and the American Indian were done beforehand. That's the only reason why I put it together. I said, all right then, here's a book, there's a reason for it.

KING: Have you ever written a poem to Neal Cassady?

CORSO: No. No. Only to Jack.

KING: Did you know Neal?

CORSO: Yeah, I knew Neal. But only to Jack, yeah. Yeah. I loved him.

KING: But Neal was another death. You know, they kind of all came in a very short period of time.

CORSO: Yeah, but they both died pretty close. You know how Neal died? He was a railroad man, worked on the railroad. In Mexico, after a wedding, he took off his clothes and walked the railroad tracks and somehow, the drinking and the cold air killed him – exposure. And then Jack went soon afterwards.

KING: You really seem attached to poetry. Several of the other writers this week have ecological concerns, or political, or scientific, but it looks like you're naked with your poetry.

CORSO: The poet and poetry is inseparable.

KING: Doesn't it get kind of cold with nothing but your poetry on?

CORSO: Oh, I've got more than that, too, you know. What is poetry but embracing the whole thing? Like I can take the megagalaxy in my head.

LITTLE: Like in "Bomb"?

CORSO: I can take the "Bomb," or I can take blue balloons. But it's not political at all. It's a death shot. You see, because people were worrying about dying by the bomb in the Fifties. So I said, what about falling off the roof, what about heart attack? And I used the double old age: old age I picked as being the heaviest – "old age, old age." One line that I've written in that poem that's not in the poem, and it should be in there is "Christ with the whip," like "St. George with a lance." I read it yesterday. I don't augment or take away, but it could be a smart idea if I did add that Christ with the whip number.

KING: Who are "old poet men" today?

CORSO: Geez, there ain't any. Really, they're gone. Auden, I'd say, was the last one probably to go.

KING: What do you think about Robert Lowell or his poetry?

CORSO: I like his "Tudor Ford," a pun, right? That kind of thing. Or the "boy with curlicues of marijuana in his hair." He's sharp. He didn't dig me too well. He dug Ginsberg because they could rap about poesy and the craft of it. When he woke up that I was in prison as a kid ... he was there for CO,[5] right ... and I was there for something else, ripping off Household Finance.

LITTLE: Tell us about the circumstances of your arrest and what it was for.

CORSO: Well, 1945, the war was over. The Army-Navy stores were selling these walkie-talkies. And I was 16 years old, right? I said "Shit, man, it would be great to get three walkie-talkies and two other guys, one guy'd be in the car saying no cops are coming along, right? We got away with 21 thou. Now I didn't know how to spend money in those days, and those guys didn't. That's how I got caught. They opened up a big hall on 99th Street, you know, Irish neighborhood. And the police asked where they got all the money. Like a dope, I gave my name to those two guys and they mentioned it. I went down to Florida and I bought a zoot suit, leaving big tips. I mean, how dopey, man alive. That's how I got to prison for three years, because the judge said I was very dangerous, that I was putting crime on a scientific basis. Those motherfuckers Household Finance, they're the ones who give you the money and take interest on it, right? I think I was a blessed man, I didn't know that. I'd have ripped off anybody, I would have done it. But I made a good shot with Household Finance.

LITTLE: Did you pick up the term "daddy" when you were in prison? Isn't it a homosexual term? What do you mean by "daddies"?

CORSO: I mean sharp people. I had no homosexual experience in prison. There was nothing like that. I was dug, though. But since I was Italian and the Mafiosi were running the shot, and I was the youngest – I entered the youngest and I left the youngest, entered 16 and a half and left 20 – I was like a little mascot. That's where I learned to be funny in life. Because I made them laugh, I was protected. Humor was a necessary survival condition when I was in prison. Man, their hearts were broken when I left prison. They dug me so fucking much … I brought life to them. There were guys doing 30–40 years. They told me, "Don't take your shoes off, Corso," in other words, "you're walking right out." And the other daddy – I didn't call them daddies then – but that other daddy said to me, "Don't *you* serve time, let time serve you." That's when I got the books, that's when the books came. Then when I left, the one man who did talk to me says, "When you're talking to six people, make sure you see seven," in other words, dig yourself. Prison food was really awful, but I had good food, because the Mafia guys got the food from the outside. They cooked steaks and everything, and I was always invited to eat.

I learned to ski in prison. Winter time comes in Plattsburgh, snow piles up. You get your skis from Sears, Roebuck. They had a ski lift going. The first time I put on a pair of ... everybody was lining up to go to their cells ... I went down beautifully, man, held myself right, and psshhh, stopped like that, took the fuckers off, got right in line to go back in. Yeah, I learned to ski in prison. I always wanted to do a play, you know, and start the play off in prison with somebody coming down on skis.

LITTLE: How come Kerouac never did deal much with homosexuality and gaiety in his books?

CORSO: Well, Jack was a beautiful, beautiful man. His sex life would have gone both ways in anything like that, you know. But then again it was more towards the female than it was anything else. But he loved his fellow man, like, he loved Neal, he loved Allen, he loved Bill Burroughs, and especially Lucien Carr. Oh wow, did you ever read Kerouac's *Vanity of Duluoz*, where his friend Lucien killed this guy who was following him in Columbia. Lucien was a very handsome young man, and this big red-haired fag was chasing Lucien all over. And Lucien finally just got tired of it, stabbed the man. The man yells out, "So this is how it happened." Not "This is how it *happens*," but "this is how it *happened*." Lucien goes with the bloody knife, up to Kerouac, who was his friend. And Jack says, "Oh, God, Lucien, Lucien." Poor Jack, man. All right, you know what he did? He helped his friend out. Dropped the knife down the sewer drain somewhere. Burroughs had the other hit, killing the wife, you know ... drunken, she puts the glass on the head ... William Tell shot, cheow. That's the weight that these people have. Burroughs told me, "Gregory, there's no such thing as an accident." So how was I going to take that?

KING: That makes Norman Mailer stabbing his wife in the arm with the scissors seem fairly small. Mailer's done a couple of things that tended to support, at least in the public eye, some things you were doing in the Fifties, "The White Negro" essay, for example.

CORSO: Well, of course, he wanted to join the bandwagon, you see. These guys who are Army writers knew where the goodies were.

KING: Do you see him much anymore? Any? At all?

CORSO: Every time I see him he wants to wrestle with me, hand wrestle. What a drag. I'll tell you, Kerouac, the football player, didn't play that shot with me. He was a strong, beautiful man; he didn't have to show his strength.

He took a Columbia University football offer and then decided he wanted to write. He meets Ginsberg and Burroughs there, right, and said, "Fuck it all." No way he's going to play football. They were just all meeting in this house, rapping all the time. Beautiful.

LITTLE: Hey, I asked you a question a while ago, and I wasn't really happy with the answer you gave me. Kerouac wrote a kind of autobiographical fiction. He wrote it just like it happened.

CORSO: Right, right, no fiction – and some of it was so beautiful.

LITTLE: Okay, then if he's writing what happened, why does he never mention gaiety, homosexuality? You've got Burroughs, Ginsberg …

CORSO: Because they never had it with Jack. Don't you understand?

LITTLE: But they had it with other people and Jack knew about it.

CORSO: Yeah, yeah, Jack knew about it, and Ginsberg loved Jack Kerouac.

LITTLE: He had to have been thinking about it. Did he censor himself?

CORSO: No. Because Jack never had homosexual affairs.

LITTLE: Why didn't he mention that he didn't?

CORSO: Why do you have to mention what you don't have?

LITTLE: Carlo[6] had it. He talked about Carlo, he described Carlo.

CORSO: That's Ginsberg. Well, Allen wasn't a rampaging faggot, you know. I told you, when I first met him he was balling that chick, Dusty Mullins.

KING: He was really with her?

CORSO: Yeah. Oh, he loved Dusty. He also loved a very fine woman, another one – what was her name – in San Francisco? Allen, funny, I guess you'll have to ask him that number – the sex shot. I don't think it's any of your affair about another person's sex life, unless you want to ask them. Don't ask me.

LITTLE: I was asking you about Kerouac's fiction technique.

CORSO: His fiction technique was very straight, it wasn't fiction. And that's what I say is so good about it.

KING: Your name, at least in the Fifties, was really connected with Ginsberg, more than any of the others we've had here this last week.

CORSO: We were the two poets. They're novelists, you know. And Allen and I were poets. When Allen and I read poetry early in those days, he would read "Howl," very serious; and I was, like I said, giving the humor number. That's what saved it. It would have been too heavy otherwise. Gregory came over with his "Marriage" or something like that, and everybody was happy and laughing. So it worked, it was a nice balance. We were the poets, Allen and myself.

KING: So really you complemented each other.

CORSO: Oh, sure, sure, sure.

KING: Ginsberg's really published a lot, has all these political connections, movement connections – he may be the most famous Beat. So you could have been in a position to say, "Gee, I wonder if I should do more things like Allen."

CORSO: Right, and I did not. I stayed out of it in the Sixties and for good reasons, too. I figured that was the route they'd taken, let them go on with it because something's going to have to happen after that; and conserve some of the energy, Gregory. Let Allen take care of it nice; and he did. You know, this man's got all his strength and his energy. You dig? I don't have to be throwing myself out like that. That's when Allen got to understand me. He was burnt up in the beginning, saying "Gregory, where are you, man, like, help us along." I said, "No, this is where you've got to understand Gregory. This is what I do now. If I'm going to go towards dope, if I'm going to make babies like I did and all that, that's my shot."

LITTLE: Tell us about meeting Ginsberg.

CORSO: Oh, that's nice. But nothing was ever planned, you dig. Nothing was planned. I met this man in a dyke bar, the Pony Stable in Greenwich Village; it was beautiful. 1950, I was about six months out of prison. I'm there with my prison poems and he just digs my face, you see, 'cause he's a homosexual, right. He didn't know who I was or my poems. Sitting down, he likes me and I says, "Well, look at these poems, you," and he says, "You got to meet a Chinaman." Now "Chinaman" was an expression meaning a second-rate poet, who was Mark Van Doren. He says, "You got to meet this poet." I says, "Oh yeah? Well, Okay, great," you know. Mark Van Doren tells me that I wrote too much about my mother. That was the critique laid on me by Mark Van Doren. John [Clellon] Holmes, who wrote *Go*, said I write too much green armpit imagery. I'm getting all these fuckers laying flak on me. All right. So finally I get Ginsberg, and I said, "Look, one thing I want to know is, I live across the street in this hotel room and I see this chick through the window balling every night, shitting, taking a bath, and I jerk off to her. I would like to go up there tonight and knock on her door and say hello to her. He says, "Oh, I'm the man you see that balls her." You dig? That's how I met Ginsberg and he brought me up there, man. It wasn't through reading the poems in a magazine somewhere and saying, "Hey, let's get together." He was the one I was jerking off to, watching him fuck her.

KING: So we know Ginsberg liked your face. What did you like about Ginsberg? Just the fact that he was an act going on across the street?

CORSO: Aw, come on. Man, he so loved me. He introduced me to Kerouac and Burroughs. He dug me a lot.

LITTLE: I'm asking what you felt towards him.

CORSO: I felt that the man dug me. Don't you understand? It was beautiful. I'm right out of prison, all right? I had those years with me. He came out of Columbia University still writing little William Carlos Williams-like poems.

KING: *Prison Poems* were even before *Vestal Lady*?

CORSO: Yeah, they're gone. They were lost in Florida. They were lost in a suitcase at Hollywood, Florida. A fucking suitcase in the Greyhound Bus Terminal. Gone. And Hope, my girlfriend – Hope, my first girlfriend – she went to all the Greyhound presidents to get the things back. Papers in a suitcase. But I remembered two poems from them, and they're in *Vestal Lady*.

"Sea Chanty." That's my first poem. See, and I remember, I don't lose nothing, man.

KING: All right.

CORSO:
My mother hates the sea,
my sea especially,
I warned her not to;
it was all I could do.
Two years later
the sea ate her.

Upon the shore I found a strange
yet beautiful food;
I asked the sea if I could eat it,
and the sea said that I could.
– Oh, sea, what fish is this
so tender and so sweet? –
– Thy mother's feet – was its answer.

Now that's a heavy because I never saw my mother. I heard that she went back to Italy, so she took the ocean, right? So that was my 16-year-old poem of someone going across the sea – but whatever goes there comes back to the shore.

KING: You never knew your mother?

CORSO: No, no. I guess I must have been about six months old when she cut out. See, I had a double whammy laid on me. When she left, they gave me to another mother, all right? Now, I thought she was my mother, and then they took me away from her. So that's like a double whammy. That was before I was two years old. So my first memory is with the second one, and you know what it is? It's a beautiful one. In the bathtub – I remember the black hair on her cunt and the water. Now that's a good shot for a two-year-old because what you got is a contemporary form of birth and that old primal shot – water.

RANKIN: How different is it now? You said that you sort of complemented Ginsberg in the old days. You were the humor and he was serious, reading "Howl." Nowadays you're still doing the same thing; you're still the humor, and yet they don't seem to tolerate you. What's happened?

CORSO: But I do write serious shots, man. But then again, I'm going to have to hold respect to Ginsberg; a little bit to Ferlinghetti, but I would hold it most to Allen.

KING: When did Peter [Orlovsky] come into all this?

CORSO: Ah, Peter – ambulance driver. He was helping people who were crashing and all that, and Allen just loved him, man; here was this guy helping people all the time. He was a beautiful man.

KING: When did he meet him?

CORSO: 1954. They've been together ever since, and they will be till they go to the happy hunting grounds. They're two good people, man. Peter's beautiful, right? Remember him today? Even though he bugs about no smoking and all that shit.

KING: He's very pure, I mean very solidly "him."

CORSO: Yeah, yeah, yeah.

KING: I don't know a lot yet about how you write a poem. There's a couple of things crossed out in "Geometric Poem" 'cause that's in your handwriting. So I don't know if you scratch out a lot, if you think a lot …

CORSO: Where's *Elegiac Feelings*? I'll show you something in it. That's a good question, that goes back to craft. See that 1940 there? [Note: Pg. 47, *Elegiac Feelings American*] I'm into the poem of Egypt when suddenly I'm bugged about President Johnson and the bombings, "the blast and the smithered," the bombs falling from the 1940s. "On the dead body of the true President," right? When Kennedy was killed? You need a magnifying glass to read it, but it's got nothing to do with the Egyptian poem. Spontaneous poetry is also spontaneous change when you're working at it. But dig my glyphs. That's the first literal translation, man. That was good, my first transliteral glyph.

KING: Is this from somewhere else that you wrote these things down?

CORSO: No, I studied for six months in Paris, I learned to do the hieroglyphs and that's a correct literal translation. Some of these things I created, though; see, this I created.

KING: That's a hippopotamus with an alligator in his mouth. [Note: Pg. 45]

CORSO: But dig my little bunny angel. She's dropping the geometry down on Egypt. Right? And then they did their triangles, right? [Note: Pg. 44]

> You O rainbow Egyp-clay
> seated upon skyey dangles
> sprinkling globes and triangles
> down upon the day

I had a ball with that.

KING: How did you learn hieroglyphics? Did you know somebody?

CORSO: Oh, six months in Paris, a M'sieur LaFrance at the Hotel Stella where Rimbaud lived. I'd get my Arab dope and I had this book from Cambridge University on hieroglyphics, and I just stayed in the room for six months all winter like that until spring. That was 1965. See, that's when I got divorced, left my wife and daughter. So I said, "Fuck it, Gregory, go off somewhere." So I went off and played around a little bit. Yeah. You know that's one that so many people like that's drawn is "The Tree." There you go. [Note: Pg. 39] Dig that. Now, the sun – Van Gogh did a beautiful thing of it. He did the tree and did the sun very big. You know that painting? It's beautiful. There's the sower in the wheat field. Now this one here I learned from prison. [Note: Pg. 38] This guy's cleaning up things. See him? All right. Now, if that ain't Egyptian … but this was where I first used the great word "scrybound." You know what "scry" means?

KING: To discern, to foretell the future …

CORSO: Right. That is what they call the guy with the crystal ball. It's "scrying"; they usually call him a swami, right? It's scry. This is where I use my music. [Note: Pg. 38]

Scrybound o'er pre-Egypt's
geometrical pool
In mine velvet robe's varium vair
– angel of darkest school

I'll descry Wlamtrice wold brool
its issuant gazebeasts
and furoak oakfur meloday
– this tenth of Atum's cursing feast

KING: There are some things there that aren't English, Gregory.

CORSO: It is English. They're old daddy words, my friend. I like to know my own language, you know. But this would be a hard poem, let's say, to read. Look at that one. [Note: Pg. 49] Here's "poet on the architect Nekhebu's knee." But you see, in the Italian edition, he's red. And there's the architect, and here's where I put myself in a shirt and tie.

KING: I was going to ask about this picture of you on this cover. You've got a tweed coat, a tie, no hair hanging down.

CORSO: Oh. The Olivetti man[7] took that picture, the man who did the Italian edition.

KING: Were you being an angel then, or something?

CORSO: I was a wild fucker, then. Are you kidding? What about the one in *Long Live Man* now, that's a nice picture of me. I was sitting next to Allen. I wished they would have kept us together there, but they took Allen out and left my picture there. That's a dreamy fucker. That was in Tangier. Then I called the book *Long Live Man*. I did that because of *Happy Birthday of Death*, and I said, "Oh God, Gregory, get off the death thing already. Say Long Live Man." I was going to do *Gregorian Rants*, but I said "I don't have to play, to entertain these people by calling my book *Gregorian Rants*."

KING: That would be almost like Pope's "Dulness," which he refused to have his book called. You don't seem to be worrying about publishing very much. Who was it, Duncan, I think, who said he wasn't going to publish anything for 15 years because he didn't want what people were expecting or anything to have any influence on him.

CORSO: Keats had that problem. See, Shelley would get along with Leigh Hunt, man, and Byron, and they'd have great raps. And Shelley was the best in it; but Keats would not join in because he didn't want to be influenced by them. And Shelley understood that – he dug Keats, you know. Shelley was a sharp daddy; oh, he's beautiful. I mean Byron couldn't stand up to him; none of them could stand up to him, when he was going good. Those meetings in the house of Leigh Hunt must have been fantastic. There are some of them written down by Mary Godwin, his wife. See, what they put down Shelley for is that he married his cousin, Harriet. She was pregnant when she threw herself in a river because he suddenly gave up on her and went towards Mary, who wrote *Frankenstein*. And so therefore, they said, there's the flaw in Shelley. No way. Harriet should have been cooler or something.

KING: One of the flaws they say is in Shelley is the line, "I fall upon the thorns of Life, I bleed," exclamation point.

CORSO: Yeah, that's a lovely line.

KING: Now, you use exclamation points.

CORSO: Right, right. I love them. That poem, "Ode to the West Wind" is one of the greatest poems ever written. You know why? It's a lyric. He smartly injected himself into it right towards the end. He said, "Make me thy lyre, even as the forest is." Right? He was always giving it to the wind but then he puts himself into it beautifully.

KING: Where'd you get this gesture of parting your hair with one finger? It really shows disdain, like on the stage at any rate, this last week. It's really been kind of a "screw the people that are trying to talk ecology."

CORSO: No, no, that's an assumption.

LITTLE: It is arrogant, and it's also elegant and feminine.

CORSO: All right. All right. And I'll take the feminine part too.

KING: You really surprised me the other day when you were reading. You said a line was too corny, like you really have an inner sense. Everybody says, "Gee, 'I fall upon thorns of Life, I bleed.' That's corny, that's sentiment, that's romantic." You're romantic, and all of a sudden you're a romantic saying, "Gee, that's too corny."

CORSO: Yeah, of course. I'm poor simple human bones.

KING: Are you hung up on being a hairy bag of water?

CORSO: Ah, that's a good one. That's what I yell on people a lot.

KING: You worried about it in the interview with Bruce Cook.[8]

CORSO: When did that happen? Oh. Oh, he lied.

KING: Well, I want to hear about Bruce Cook.

CORSO: Mr. Cook was a liar. I'll tell you about him. See, when I was living in New York City, he said I was sleeping in a sleeping bag. Bullshit! I was with Belle [Carpenter]. Now, I didn't know she was a DuPont lady, you dig. I mean, wow, what a house we had. She was an Aries, like me. On the floors there were big fucking rams.

KING: He said you could just leave any day, man.

CORSO: Yeah, of course. But there was the most elegant fucking house, man. Her father knocked out these lions; there were all these lions on the floor, rugs and everything, man. Shit, that dummy wanted to create something; he said, "Well, Gregory, that little beatnik, with his sleeping bag." I never slept in a sleeping bag … beautiful fucking bed there, man.

KING: Have you read that book?

CORSO: Yeah, I thought it sucked because he lied.

LITTLE: What lies?

CORSO: Well, the visit to the house. The only time he met me was at the house with me and Belle. We served him nice drinks in the garden and everything.

Shit. He didn't mention that. He had me sleeping in a sleeping bag. Bullshit. Do you think it's an insult that I call human beings hairy bags of water?

KING: I don't think so from where it comes from; I mean we're a sack of guts. That's what people are.

CORSO: That's what I mean, right. That's what they are. You see, and it's a chemical hit. That's going to save them. Their bodies are all perfect, beautiful. I love fucking and all that. You are a hairy bag of water, aren't you?

KING: You talk a lot about death.

CORSO: Oh, I took death when I was a happy kid, man. Man, I took death in 1957, my death shot. I was a happy guy. I said, "Now tackle it, Corso; take the biggies." I'm no morbid soul.

KING: Are you not worried about death now?

CORSO: Oh, hell, no. I passed that shot. I told you in that poem on the airplane, I scared the guy more than the plane. And when he thanked me for it, I said, "Look, I passed that death fear shot a long time ago." You know how I passed it? In 1960 in Luxembourg Gardens in Paris, Sunday afternoon, people with their perambulators and children, old people sitting on the park benches, children pulling their boats in the pond there, lovers kissing on the grass. I said, "This is heaven, Gregory." Suddenly behind a tree I saw a guy with an axe, and I said, "Boy, he could make a shambles of this heaven – chop, chop, chop." Now who put that man behind the tree? I did; he wasn't there. But he *is* there in life, isn't he? That fucker is there with your bombs or whatever you call it. I called that heaven, the way things were going there. I saw the shambles of it, chop, chop, chop. It don't mean nothing to me, that chop, chop, chop – no more. And what about you – what about you people? Now would you get scared if you felt your heart was feeling pattering and suddenly you turned pale? And you might just have a heart attack and drop dead here? I think I'd go to a movie theater. I would. If I felt that was happening I'd run into a movie house.

KING: Why a movie house?

CORSO: I don't know … I thought I'd just get my mind off it or something.

Can I ask you a question, John? Are you a happy man?

LITTLE: Right now, yeah.

CORSO: I want to build up to something. Do you feel there are any mysteries? Something you don't understand?

LITTLE: I don't worry about them, wonder about them.

CORSO: All right. Do you have any enemies?

LITTLE: I don't worry much about it if I do.

CORSO: I don't have any; I make them all into friends, you know. All right. Do you love me?

LITTLE: I believe I do, and I think I loved you on first sight. You know, you got off that goddamn airplane with your fucking gold earrings, your long hair, your purple shirt, and you ran around hugging people and frightening old ladies. Let me ask my question; I'm going to ask you one. I want you to give us a chronological and exact history of your use of drugs, related to what you were writing at the time, when you first began using them, when you finished, and the effect that they had.

CORSO: Okay. I took drugs after the poetry was written. I took drugs very late. I started in 1963; I was 33 years old.

LITTLE: Never in prison, never before prison?

CORSO: No. I smoked pot in 1950 when I came out of prison. That's a joint every now and then. But I saw people shooting up. I never took the heavies then. In 1956 especially in Mexico, the marijuana was real good. But in 1963 – heroin; that was the weight. I took it to experiment with my head and I forgot one thing. You said the arrogance of this gesture – I forgot that. Boy, if you get stuck on some fuck like that, then you got to give in. And that was very rough for a guy like me. I had to go beg for that fucker. So I said then it's nobody's business, Gregory – that's my medicine in the medicine cabinet, my chemistry. But I dropped it; I don't have to take drugs now.

LITTLE: Well, do you take methadone?

CORSO: No.

LITTLE: How long have you been off methadone?

CORSO: Methadone I've been off now two days. When I was in New York recently I was taking drugs again, heroin. Now, if I just stop and don't take methadone I would have to go a few days real cold turkey, and I don't dig it. But if you just take a little bit of methadone, ten milligrams, not the hundred milligrams they give these guys, you can gradually be off it again, you dig? And that's why I go into drinking. A person takes drugs doesn't drink. I drink, right? And I've been feeling pretty good. I got great recuperative powers.

LITTLE: Can you write when you take drugs?

CORSO: No, no.

LITTLE: Are you going to quit? Are you going to get off drugs in order to do this big number you got planned?

CORSO: It's already done, this next book.

LITTLE: You were on drugs when you did it?

CORSO: Ahhh, no. It's an alien substance in you. It knocked out the spirit of me. I didn't bother writing. What I dug doing with it was fucking because it erects your dick a long time. It takes a long time for you to come. So poetry was out of it. And when the poetry came, and I say it's a rare little number, this little brick musehouse that I've been doing, when it came it was intermittent. It was ... well, I said, "Corso, is this a drag now to get the money to buy the dope and I'm being a pain in the ass among my friends by getting the money – so cool it." See, I'm no liar.

LITTLE: Okay. How is your taking drugs and what you experienced when you take drugs – how much of that goes into your poetry?

CORSO: I don't take drugs to write about drugs. It's been done, right?

KING: What about Lawrence Lipton's *Holy Barbarians*?[9] Did you ever feel a sense of responsibility or connection with those Venice West people?

CORSO: As far as responsibility, I have none. Not me, no way. That's an early book, isn't it? He was talking about people like me, right?

KING: I think he was talking about, you know, like you get a movement and you get five poets or three poets to do something and there's an intellectual and emotional validity and spiritual validity, even. And all of a sudden there's a thousand people doing some of the things those people did, but not the other half.

CORSO: I don't know about the other half. He saw me and Allen Ginsberg; we all came from the East to San Francisco, and this man, who just used to write about communist literature – all that shit! – was very, very impressed by us. It was early in the game. I don't know how it fits, or what.

LITTLE: Hey, do you care very much about ecology?

CORSO: Should I? I don't know … I mean I don't *not* care, you dig what I mean? My daughter cares.

KING: How old is she?

CORSO: Ten years old. Yeah, she really cares. I stopped her from killing also. When she was a kid, she was about to stomp on a bug. I said, "No way." She never then killed anything. But I caught her, man, when she was about to fink on me. She was going to go tell her mommie in the other room that I was lighting up a cigarette and I said, "What? No way you tell on your father." "But I don't care. That's wrong, daddy, what you're doing is wrong." And she tells me to get fake teeth also.

KING: Where is she now?

CORSO: New York City. She just can't stand graffiti, she's so protected. She's an angel. When she sees graffiti, it really upsets her. So I said to the mother, "Well, man, I gotta be around her a little to wake this kid up fast, man. I don't want it to give her a jolt, when she gets this one shot, you know, what life is. You could easily let it grow in her, man."

KING: What does her mother say?

CORSO: Well, her mother's beginning to check me out and realize that I'm right. She's a little overprotective with the kid.

LITTLE: You ever think about your three-year-old who's going to read your poems someday?

CORSO: Yeah. Well, she's the angel – blonde hair and blue eyes. Her family made the atom bomb, and I wrote the "Bomb" poem. See the combine? The DuPont people were the first ones to make the atom bomb. The mother is DuPont and the daddy is the one who wrote the "Bomb" poem. So my daughter goes around and can say, "Well, okay. If they made the bomb, look what my daddy did."

KING: The two consciousnesses …

CORSO: Right. And that was no choice. It just happened. And Belle, beautiful. Belle is beauty, right? And she is very beautiful. Boy, she's strong and tough. Those New Mexican people, I'm telling you, man alive.

KING: Those who?

CORSO: People in New Mexico like they were mentioning up on the stage today.

KING: How does that tie up with New Mexico?

CORSO: Oh, female. Oh, because they live there, my daughter and Belle.

LITTLE: The three-year-old.

CORSO: Three-year-old, right. But you know it's good that I have two daughters rather than, I feel, a guy because what a weight to lay on a boy, right – me? The son always tries to knock out the daddy.

KING: The girls can incorporate it more.

CORSO: Oh, yeah, I heard yesterday that the Women's Lib in town got to dig me. They were pissed off with me in the beginning. Reason they got to dig me was that I did say to them very straight, "Poets have been taking the whole shot all the time, you can't make a dichotomy. You can't just take half of it; you got to take the whole number. That'll save it, that'll do it."

KING: What happened between like when you were 10 and 17? Where were you?

CORSO: Ten to 17; that's good, a decade shot. One to 10, I had eight mothers, because I didn't have my mother; they sent me to all these orphanages and foster homes. Ten to 17 were really funny years 'cause 16 and a half – prison, 13 – bad boys' home; so from 10 to 17 – institutional; out on the streets when I was 20 years old. I slept on the rooftops and in the subways of New York, man. I had no home. From 11 years old to 16 and a half.

KING: Do you speak Italian?

CORSO: I could understand my father talk it; my grandmother, I used to understand her.

KING: Do you know other languages?

CORSO: Ancient Egyptian. Not spoken much today.

KING: Ancient Egyptian. You'll never get into the Peace Corps, I tell you. You must look up a lot of etymology in dictionaries, like where it refers you to another word to another word to another word?

CORSO: Oh, I used to. See, I know words – beautiful words from the past that people don't know, and it really saves the words. For instance, "scry" we got before; we understand what "scry" is. A pentacle maker – you know who he is?

KING: No.

CORSO: Karcist. K-A-R-C-I-S-T. Okay, that's one for you. Now, the wind, that goes through the trees. You know what it is? Murmur, right? It's an onomatopoeic shot. You know what it really is? B-R-O-O-L.

KING: In Old English?

CORSO: Yeah. Thomas Carlyle, really. Poets can create onomatopoeia if they want, like "the duck quacked." I mean, my great little drawing of a duck, and out of the mouth comes "onomatopoeia"; I don't go "quack" with the duck. I could sell that little cartoon to *The New Yorker*, I bet. I mean, it's a great one, right, a duck going "onomatopoeia." And I just love "duck" – I love the word, "duck." They're funny, ducks, man.

KING: Did you read Philip Lamantia? Because you've got some images which really get into surrealism.

CORSO: Yeah, yeah, him early, and André Breton; I dug him when I was 14 years old. Philip, now, you're talking about the guy who I dig a lot.

KING: A lot of your images are really surrealistic: "a wrinkled angel weeping axle grease" or something like that, which is getting close to surrealism.

CORSO: "Wrinkled angels," yet. I have to go back and read my poetry and learn. I love putting words together like "wheels of rainlight," "treelight."

KING: You put words together. Like Kerouac.

CORSO: Oh, yeah, that's compound, that is like chemistry. You put iron and another element together and you get a third. So that gives the birth, right? And when you put the heavies like "sex death" together, what do you get? You put two together, you do get a third. One and one does make three. Now, where four comes from always grabs me; really suspicious about four. I was playing around with geometry, but that's a big daddy, the number four. *Uno, uno,* and the baby out is the third, right? Who's that fourth fucker?

KING: That's the guy with the axe.

CORSO: (*Laughing*) The guy with the axe.

INTERVIEW: GREGORY CORSO

Fred Misurella

Gregory Corso, who along with Allen Ginsberg, Lawrence Ferlinghetti, and Jack Kerouac was one of the four principal leaders of the Beat Movement in the 1950s, is writing poems and having babies in Paris. Older, although still not subdued, Corso is one of the few contemporary writers of whom it can be said he had truly influenced his time in social, as well as literary, terms. In Gasoline, The Happy Birthday of Death, *and other books, Corso questioned the bourgeois, money-making conformity of the Eisenhower era, and through his example helped open up the alternative lifestyles that gave birth to the youth movement of the 1960s.*

Frequently compared to Shelley by literary critics, his poetry has a whimsical, prophetic quality that emphasizes feeling as opposed to intellectual restriction, and individual liberty as opposed to social norms. Along with Ginsberg and Ferlinghetti, Corso has also made the stuff of modern technological society a part of this poetry – thus the title of his book, Gasoline *– and in his present work he is attempting to combine the acceptance of technological change in the modern world with the necessity of finding, as he calls it, "something immutable" underneath that change which is basic and everlasting. A modern romantic, he has been associated with the fringes of society for most of his career, but he hastens to say that he attended Harvard University as a student and has taught in various American universities.*

Corso lives in an apartment in the 16th[1] with a young French-American woman named Jocelyn [Stern] and their new child, Max-Orpheo Kerouac Corso. Fred Misurella interviewed the poet at his apartment recently and found him in a singularly anti-French mood. The excerpts follow.

MISURELLA: You've been working on a book for the last four years, you said.

CORSO: Yes. It's called *Heirlooms from the Future*.[2] It's almost done. Heirlooms means two things: it means a gift given from the past to the present; and it's also a rug that's worked out to be symmetrically perfect. I want the book to be symmetrically perfect – the poems and all that. So the title has a double meaning.

MISURELLA: Have you changed much since your last poems? Does this book show any difference in your writing style?

CORSO: No. As I am within, so it comes out on the paper. The only thing that can change is the ideas – the content, say, over political things. But feelings express themselves the same as they always have. Style has never been a problem for me.

MISURELLA: Your poetry has always seemed playful to me. Would you agree?

CORSO: Well, it's tough play. It can be play. With a serious subject the play will come in handy. Like with clichés – I use a lot of clichés intentionally, so that there's a double force. Humor is for the tough shots, that is to get across the truth. Let's say that to get rid of a lie you use humor. Especially with Americans – if they can laugh at something, then that gets rid of the thing they're laughing at. If it becomes laughable, it can no longer exist as it was in its serious state. So humor is a very powerful shot. It's what I call a Divine Butcher – it gets rid of all the bullshit.

MISURELLA: A lot of good American literature is humorous. Do you think that might be part of the American personality?

CORSO: Yes. It makes readers accept things, things they already know about, because you can't make people accept things they don't already know. What you can do for them is enlighten them. They say, "Oh, yeah. Of course I already knew this." So all you're doing is lighting up something in their heads. Humor does that. Now if they see something that is obscure, it's because the poet is being obscure and is not lighting up anything in their heads.

MISURELLA: So you don't believe in obscurity then – you think it's the poet's fault if the poem is obscure?

CORSO: Yeah. You see, there are poets who go after what I call "nonexistent unknowables." Nobody is ever going to get them, because they don't exist. But there are existing unknowables, and once a poet hits upon them, then they become known to other people – the readers. That's what you call illumination.

MISURELLA: So you're not talking about the grand things – the big questions like death and love – when you talk about nonexistent unknowables?

CORSO: No. Those are existing unknowables. That's why they've always been major themes for poets. But there are some who go seeking to circle the square – or square the circle, and you can never get what they're after.

MISURELLA: What about religion?

CORSO: Some get into the religious aspect – like Ginsberg. He's mainly into a religious shot, about how people themselves can be healthy through their own seekings, the things they were confused by. Because especially in America they never had their own god; it was always imported. That's why that country's god-sick. They get these people like Moon[3] over there, or Satchidananda,[4] and they grab them in America because they're god-sick, they have no god. The Indians had the gods, but the so-called white man imported his. So those that are born in the States now have no real god that's their own. Or the continent's.

MISURELLA: That's an interesting point. In other words it's a sort of a European god that was …

CORSO: Yeah, brought over, and it knocked over the Indian god. And the country's suffering for that today because of pollution and whatnot. The American Indian respected the ground that he walked on. He did not defile it. His gods taught him that. Their great gods were the sky and the air you breathe. When the Indian dies, he never would bury the body because it would defile the earth; he never would burn it because it would defile fire and the air. He wouldn't put it in water because it would defile water. So he left it up on a high cliff and let the birds eat it. Or a high platform that they built. But the so-called white man didn't have those gods, and as a result America has become what I call "god-sick." The Asians come over with their philosophy – Zen, for example – which is a very sharp philosophy – but it's not American.

MISURELLA: Are you still in contact with people like Ginsberg?

CORSO: Oh sure. Constantly. I was just with him last year. I was teaching with him in the Naropa Institute in Colorado. Allen was just here visiting me a couple of months ago. And Ferlinghetti – he's supposed to be coming by soon. If he is, he'll probably get in touch with me, because he knows where I am. But I never made the scene too much with poets. I'm invited to a lot of readings, but I never pushed myself too much. Especially in the Sixties. That was a time of hiatus in America, where it was getting into what you can call the Beat Movement. It was coming to the fore, socially, only they called it the Hippie movement. But it was basically the same thing.

MISURELLA: Can you expand on that a bit.

CORSO: That's what a movement does. It changes. What was predicted by Kerouac, in *On the Road* particularly, of youth coming to the fore, of going on the road, of traveling with rucksacks through America, of finding themselves, or taking drugs; a lot of them sought, either in their heads or physically, to make a journey. And in the Sixties that came to fore and was expressed a lot through music. But music was all it gave. It didn't give you much intelligence, or much education. I mean the Hippies weren't as educated as the Beats were. The Beats were knowledgeable, they had gone to the universities and whatnot, whereas most of these kids would just go to Woodstock and kiss naked and smoke pot and listen to rock music. If they picked out one philosophical line from Bob Dylan it was like big news. Now that the Seventies are here – I found this out when I was at the Naropa Institute in Boulder – now they're all suddenly wanting to open up their heads in order to learn. They want to find the sources – the basics of things.

MISURELLA: That's what seems to be happening in the Seventies.

CORSO: That's what the Seventies are all about. That's something you can only find out in the middle of the decade; you couldn't see in the beginning of the Seventies because no one knew exactly where it was going. Now we see – the Seventies are where people are mainly checking themselves out, asking where their sources are.

MISURELLA: And how has this affected you, if I may ask?

CORSO: Well, I'm an elder. Like I say, there's four years' work sitting on the desk. It's the culmination of what I feel is going to be in the Seventies and after. When I say "heirlooms from the future" I mean to say what is coming and what is going to be. It will be beneficial – through the expression of the poetry anyway – to those who read it. The readers then take the torch and carry it on. The poet can only suggest the paths that are open in the future. One doesn't suggest that you take drugs or try mescaline – that's all been laid out already. That was appropriate for a particular period in life. And a lot of them had to pay for it too. Timothy Leary had to pay for the message by going to jail. (*Laughter*)

MISURELLA: There seem to be quite a few people who were protesting in the Sixties and early Seventies now going back to America. Like Eldridge Cleaver.[5]

CORSO: They're tired of being exiles. At one time that was the thing to do. Now he figures, probably, that if he goes back and renounces what he's done, he can get a fair shake. And maybe he will, because, what can he renounce anyway? Like when they say Leary was finking for the FBI for him to get out of jail. Who could he tell on anyway? What can he tell? That somebody took acid? (*Laughter*) Big deal. Who's that going to get into trouble? All they want to do is discredit Leary by it, so that people will say down with Leary and down with what he stands for. See, this probably was the agreement that he had with the FBI. All right, he probably said, make me into this no-good fink and I'll get free. Ginsberg and I figured it must have been like that.

MISURELLA: There was a book of interviews called *Allen Verbatim*[6] and I remember how interesting it was in the ending where Ginsberg is in his farmhouse, very withdrawn and talking about getting into himself. Is this a sign of where he's at now?

CORSO: Yeah. That happened in Cherry Valley. He had just broken his leg. Poor guy slipped on the ice when he went out to get some water. I was there. We had to drag him back into the house and call an ambulance. Allen's very accident prone. So he was withdrawing then, but now is a different time. Now he's acting like a groupie, with Dylan. Wherever Dylan is, he's there.
　　Allen always gets these things from people. Like if he shaves off his

beard it becomes a big piece of news. "Why did he shave off his beard?" everybody asks. "It must be symbolic." Why? Well, if anybody like Dylan tells him to shave off his beard, he shaves it off. That's why he did it. Dylan said, "Shave your beard off," and Allen said, "Sure" and he shaved it off. Then people go around saying, "Oh, there must be some big significance behind it. Allen is changing." (*Laugher*) Weird, right? I mean what hair can mean, what can it suggest to people?

MISURELLA: Well, I got the idea from *Allen Verbatim* that he was getting into himself for a specific reason.

CORSO: Well, Martin Buber[7] told him that. That's why. He was giving too many readings. He was too active. He had to close off for a while. And so he got into meditating and all that in order to get deeper into himself. It cooled him out a lot.

MISURELLA: He seems to see himself as a sort of prophet, doesn't he?

CORSO: People see him as that. He's a very active man; he can't stay put for any length of time. During the protest marches in Washington he was always there OM-ing away in order to cool the scene down. Which he did a lot. And, as I say, the Seventies are a lot quieter. People don't have as much to complain about. There's no war to complain about, no Nixon to kick around anymore. (*Laugher*) The economy seems to be changing now so that more people are getting jobs, so a change seems to be happening.

MISURELLA: I always got the impression in reading about Ginsberg that during the Fifties he was everybody's agent – the Beats, anyhow. Is that true?

CORSO: He was very talkative about people he liked and that way he promoted them. But none of us were really alike. Kerouac and Burroughs were two different kinds of novelists. Myself and Ginsberg are very different. The Beat Movement was very varied. That was one of the main things that held us together, the fact that we could all be different and still like each other's stuff. That happened to be the right time to be a poet. Anybody could get published then because we were looking for new stuff. Today it's very difficult. Before the Fifties it was difficult, too. In those days things were much more open. The opening occurred in Frisco mainly, with Ferlinghetti's City Lights, but the northeastern establishment was – and still is – closed.

MISURELLA: Let me ask you some things about America and France and their relationship. Are you going to stay here in preference to America?

CORSO: No, no. America is a place I'll always go back to. I dug France when I first came here in 1957; it was a real swinging time. I didn't come back here for 20 years. I heard in America that France has changed, that it's dead and isn't as lively as it used to be, and I never took that too seriously from people because I figured that maybe they, not the country, had changed. But somehow it wasn't like that. I realized that the place did change; it wasn't as gassy as it used to be. You could sense it in the atmosphere. Culturally something has gone out of the country. You can feel the absence.

MISURELLA: Would you say that the Paris scene is no longer important?

CORSO: Well, I can't say that it's bad. Things have changed, that's all. If we compare Paris to New York City, you can see the difference. There, things change, but there's something that's always immutable there, and that would be the tendency toward culture, toward something being beautiful and all that. And I no longer find it here. It's not even here in the young people. You get a feeling here that the country will be down on you for any artistic endeavor. I always remember that this is a country of the bourgeois. So really its artistic reputation was always a big con. The arts was only a few people at a time. The main people were always the bourgeoisie – the shopkeepers, the workers – not the artists. Its reputation comes from the fact that they gave birth to so many artists – good artists – that made it be known. But look, they're closing down the Opera. It can't afford to keep itself going. What are the tourists going to come to this country for in the future? They come to see the beauty, but the buildings they come to see are the ones they're knocking down – Les Halles[8] for instance. I think there's a malaise of feeling here. I get that feeling here. I've been born and raised in cities and I know them well. There's something that's wrong with Paris. I know New York City to be a heavy mother – oh boy, is it heavy! But nonetheless something is always happening there. You can go from one area to another and it's different – not like Paris where every neighborhood is always the same.

MISURELLA: You sound very negative about Paris. How do you see America at this point?

CORSO: Oh, I think America is great. There's always a renewal. But I feel that better when I get away from it. The farther away I get, the better perspective I have on it.

MISURELLA: Is it the people? The political institutions? Or what?

CORSO: No, no. It's not the political situation; that's always fucked up. It's in the people that are coming. There is always something new; there's always some new ground being broken. Here you can't even break the language. They have an academy that keeps the language perfect, whereas America is always giving birth to new sounds, new words to express things more. Then they pick up on the words here. This country just isn't as creative today as it was 20 years ago. It wasn't as industrial as it is now. But while they've gone a long way economically, they haven't kept up artistically.

MISURELLA: Do you think you could say the same thing about America? We've always been number one industrially, but I wonder about artistically.

CORSO: Not "we," man, not "we." You're talking about the politicians. The people are different. In America you can always say "Fuck the flag" and nobody says anything. You just try that here. In the States you get your vibes from talking to people. You know who you're talking to and what you can say. Not here. But let me just say, I dig France. It gave me a lot. I wrote some of my best poems here.

MISURELLA: Where did you live?

CORSO: A hotel behind the Git-le-Cœur, right behind Boulevard Saint-Michel. Burroughs was there at the time too. Ginsberg was there as well. It was called the Beat Hotel.

MISURELLA: Do you see any writers who come through here anymore?

CORSO: The ones I know. I don't see young ones anymore, because they don't have anything to say. A young writer has to be like Rimbaud for me to feel he's got something to say. I just don't think poetry is in this country anymore. The atmosphere is very tight here and it's taking the poetry away.

MISURELLA: I'd like to quarrel a little bit with that. I don't always feel free in America. It depends on who I'm talking to.

CORSO: It's always like that. You got to know who you're talking to. I know that I have complete freedom through giving readings and talks. I know I always have complete freedom. I have not suffered in America for what I've done. I've always felt most free in America.

MISURELLA: Did you feel that during the Nixon years? The Johnson years?

CORSO: Oh, yeah. Especially those years because it was so ridiculous. I felt unfree in the Kennedy years because those were the years when the politicians were trying to tell us "We'll take care of everything. We got things happening now. We're sending men up to the moon, etc. You people can just take it easy now." The Johnson years were great opening years because that's when everybody started to question the government. Then that opened up the universities and got the young going out and participating in government decisions saying, "We don't want this shit. We don't want his war."

MISURELLA: I'm sure you didn't feel this during the McCarthy era, the Joe McCarthy era.

CORSO: The McCarthy era was the one time that I exerted myself to see how free I could be. That's when the whole Beat thing started, in the Fifties. When McCarthy came along we started opening our mouths. This is an American tradition – it goes back through the Wobblies and the Bohemians in the Twenties and Thirties – people are always opening their mouths and telling the government to stop. This often happened in questions of economy – the questioning of poverty. You had them who were the intellectuals questioning, or you had them who were gangsters robbing banks. But the literary traditions in America – like with Pound and W.C. Williams – were interested in getting at America's roots, not its foreign, European ones – not the ones that were English. They wanted to write American, not English, literature. What they didn't realize was that it was automatically going to happen, that the children of the immigrants were going to automatically speak American, not English.

MISURELLA: A lot of Kerouac's work represents an attempt to go back ...

CORSO: And find his sources. Right. That's a message I always gave, as a poet and as a teacher. Check out your sources. Find out where you came from. Then you know where you're going. That's why I call my new book *Heirlooms from the Future.*

POETRY POWER FOR A BLOODLESS COUP: AN INTERVIEW WITH GREGORY CORSO
Tom Plante

Back in the San Francisco Bay area after a long absence, Corso is staying in Oakland at the home of poets Linda and Andy Clausen. The following interview occurred on September 15, 1977, as Corso fixed pancakes after a sleepless night with his son, Max, who was teething.

PLANTE: Why are you in the Bay Area?

CORSO: I just finished a summer tenure at the Naropa Institute in Boulder, Colorado, where Andy Clausen suggested a San Francisco reading. I said "great," because I haven't read here since the early Beat days, 21 years ago.

PLANTE: When were you last in the area?

CORSO: Around 1968, at the time of the Haight-Ashbury's last throes.

PLANTE: Why haven't you read here since then?

CORSO: Nobody suggested a reading, that's why.

PLANTE: You taught a course on Shelley at Buffalo, New York?

CORSO: Right, in 1964. I was fired for not taking the loyalty oath.[1] The students demonstrated on my behalf and they knocked out the loyalty oath. I taught a general poetry course at Albuquerque, New Mexico, before coming to Frisco in 1968. Before Naropa, I was in Europe a year and a half.

Paris is like what Berkeley was like 20 years ago. Nowhere. Now Berkeley is still nowhere. It's gone downhill, but it was uphill in the Sixties and early Seventies, a lot of noise.

PLANTE: Governor Reagan and tuition changed that.

CORSO: There's nothing to get up in arms about. But if there was, Berkeley would come to the fore, even if the select students here aren't proletarian. Will Berkeley rise again and lead the other U.S. colleges? Yes. But we have to bring back the bums, agitators, fiends, maniacs and neo-Platonists. I know that sounds like a motley bunch and they probably couldn't do squat if they tried.

The real power lies with the teachers. It's for them to wake up the students. All this without any violence is the only way we're gonna get somewhere. It's time for the economists to carry the standard of blessed provocation.

PLANTE: Now there seems to be more neighborhood focus.

CORSO: The goodies squeezed from the pain of the past. I'd like to see what the freshmen will produce four years from now. Everywhere I've been, like Europe and all, they look to Berkeley. If it's happening here, it's happening in the country. This area is a birthplace, Frisco for poetry and Berkeley for subtle revolutionary change. The revolution happened and there were changes. Now people are reflecting. There's got to be a perpetual change or a stagnant, deplorable lot will graduate four years from now.

PLANTE: What about the mass media's emphasis on sensationalism?

CORSO: The wave of change will get across, not the mass murders. The media doesn't create change. They see change and jump in to be part of it. Nothing good has come out of the Hearst Press. Media like that is one of America's big black stains. They become the illustrious obscure, like Walter Winchell.

PLANTE: Was he an early Walter Cronkite?

CORSO: Cronkite has class. Winchell was a gossip columnist in the Forties and he could make or break people. The power heads caused no good at all.

I'm 47. I read the papers in the Forties. It was sensationalism for a gullible public. It was the poor that suffered. The Hearst papers were jury and judge, calling criminals "mad dogs." They never had a chance. Communists became the next scapegoat because Hearst and Scripps-Howard needed headlines. J. Edgar Hoover didn't go after the Mafia, but the communists. This country was led into darkness by the supposed righteous. In the Fifties, Senator Joe McCarthy was finally exposed. The Beats exposed everything, all laid bare.

Blessed be the poets, the one so-called unacknowledged power that nobody can mess with.

PLANTE: What about the social-climber poets?

CORSO: If they have poetry, great. If they don't, they can't destroy poetry. It's the soul and voice of people. It's an eternal shot.

PLANTE: What about bad poetry?

CORSO: Bad poetry is a crime. Bank robbing is noble compared to bad poetry. When the Beats came about, children of immigrants and street people, bad poets said, "If they can do it, so can we." And it weakened at the time. But the essence is with us today.

If people write poetry, then it's a good spark. Like there's good and bad architecture. People live in and rent the bad, but to look at it? Same with revolution. What did people expect? A bloodbath? It doesn't happen that way here. It's sophisticated and continuous, not like a junta takeover. The less bloodshed the better. Beat was a revolution and it spilled no blood. Beats gave birth to hippies and still spilled no blood.

There'll be no next planned move. It'll happen on its own accord. South Africa won't provide the impetus, but it's a heavy weight. The wave of the future may be in the head of someone as yet unborn. And don't expect rock and roll to do it. Tin gods and entertainment. Rock and rollers know this, but others call them poets. Anyone tells me the Bee Gees are poets then I'm just going to say nothing. It's too absurd to answer that.

PLANTE: What about punk rock?

CORSO: "Punk" could mean something if it extends itself away from the rock moneymakers. Now, punk poetry – maybe something solid there. What's a punk? A young person. The best poetry is written by the young.

Not the swaggering, arrogant wise-ass. Punk is an attitude. The punk has to be educated. It must encompass environment and the world around us. High class punk.

Like Rimbaud was punk. He stepped on toes indiscriminately. And François Villon. But punk rock? It's just advancing careers in entertainment, the old Hollywoodian bag. That's why I'm reading with Andy Clausen. He's coming to the fore after living punk for years. I'm getting on and haven't been called punk in years, since prison. Daddy punk and Andy punk.

PLANTE: You're reading with them because they're punks?

CORSO: No, because they're good poets. Call them punk or whatever you want. They're good poets. I'm tired of reading with the old mob, even though I don't give many readings. I haven't read because the time wasn't opportune. But I've been writing and I'll have something to say. Now, Allen Ginsberg is always active, making bread for the funds that help other people. But I don't like people to hear my inner feelings read aloud. Read the books.

PLANTE: What do you see for the future?

CORSO: Youth is sharper in the Seventies. Students should prove Reagan wrong; show they have the fire and youth will not be sieved. They're all one, in the same leaky lifeboat.

PLANTE: Do you believe in 1984?

CORSO: No. I won't presume what the Eighties will bring, but it's bound to be better. Through the Sixties "power" finally became a good word, when people took it, like gay power, black power; before that, there was only creepy power. My "Power" poem, written in Frisco in 1956, aimed at changing power. It was called fascistic, but it was intended to benefit people, not hurt them.

The poet that just benefits himself won't make it for long. Keats said the poet is God's spy. President Carter – the old religion – they just run the American shuttle. There's no Baptist Church in Proxima Centauri.

PLANTE: What about North Beach in San Francisco?

CORSO: North Beach never was what people thought. Jack Kerouac's novel, *The Subterraneans*, was New York. Kerouac made North Beach happen. But

Michael McClure and Philip Lamantia and others were already there. So what is North Beach? City Lights Books and coffee houses? A desperation home away from home? Hippie-Dippies?

PLANTE: What about Bob Kaufman's window-smashing "Sputnik?"[1]

CORSO: What about it? Next to Ginsberg and me, in Paris, Bob Kaufman is the most appreciated American poet. And he's translated a lot. I told him in the Fifties, "Be funny." Thus his humor spared him.

PLANTE: What about the poetry quibblers?

CORSO: I'm not into quibblers. Don't gripe about Ferlinghetti; do your thing. Don't put the weight on him even if he put that publishing task on himself.

PLANTE: What do you think about the San Francisco poets?

CORSO: I like poets like Philip Lamantia. Workers like Andy Clausen. Philip Whalen I like, but not poets that fall into religion. The poet has to be god of his own religion and doctor of his own head.

The replicas of Ginsberg or anybody – and I hear there are 10,000 around here – are Xerox copies. They'll never make it as bona fide poets. The essential thing is to find your own spirit and voice, without knocking your predecessors.

Any poet that can't take another poet saying his stuff stinks isn't a poet. A poet has to know he's a poet.

THE RIVERSIDE INTERVIEWS: 3
GREGORY CORSO

Gavin Selerie

INTRODUCTION

The interview that forms the first half of this book[1] was recorded, under somewhat bizarre circumstances, at the house of Jay Landesman in late September, 1980. A few days earlier, Corso had given an inspired reading at the Poetry Olympics in Westminster Abbey[2], and afterwards he had agreed to contribute to the interview series before his actual reading at Riverside Studios on October 3rd. When we talked later on the phone he suggested that it might be preferable to talk at the place where he was staying and that, if I was agreeable, we should do the interview that very evening. Although I felt ill-prepared to conduct a high-level discussion and was tired after a full working day, I was aware that the chance might not present itself again and acquiesced. A slightly odd note was sounded in Corso's closing remark: "You're gonna take me to a restaurant afterward, right? I give you the interview shot, you buy me a £10 meal." While not unreasonable, this bargain set the tone for an exchange which at times seemed more of a market dispute than a sensitive investigation of poetics. Still, I said, this is one of the people who hit me the strongest when I was young and I'm curious to find what has become of him. There had been a long silence during the Seventies and now Corso appeared to be writing with renewed vigour and authority.

When I arrived in Islington bearing the brandy which had been requested by "a penniless living legend" (as Corso himself put it), I found the household in some disarray. Jay Landesman and Corso were engaged in a conversation which seemed to be going nowhere and deep booming sounds from the basement were vying with an operatic overture for supremacy of mood. I sat around the small circular table and for a few minutes my presence was scarcely acknowledged. I gathered that Landesman was about to depart and that the music downstairs was being played by his son, Miles, whose 18th (?) birthday was at hand. It was, you might say, a typical beat pad: large double bed on the floor serving as further seating space, heavy rugs and drapes, a kitchen area flung far back but open to view.

Corso was smashed – appealingly loose but slightly demonic. The wicked angel I had previously envisaged, scowling and grinning by turns. Deeply lined face, eyes sunk back but boring through your gaze, hair an electric sweep of silver. The stage was set for a sparring match. It struck me that I had not had the opportunity to reread his work, but it seemed that the occasion might be fresher for this lack of forethought. I had heard much of Corso's new material in the Abbey and numerous questions bubbled at the door of consciousness – not least, the issue of Corso's allegiance to a kind of poetics that was vastly different from Olson's. In the event I didn't get the opportunity to voice many of the feelings I had concerning Corso's art, I was pushed into an intellectual corner like the hapless student reporter in *Dont Look Back*.[3] However, after Landesman had left, we got down to some strong talk and what emerged was, if chaotic and dispersed, still deeply revealing. You don't talk with Corso like you do with Ginsberg or Ferlinghetti, the one studiously dynamic, the other courteously articulate. Corso is a man jealous of his stature, a tough customer who retains the zest and relentless individuality of his urban youth. Whatever he is thinking you'll know it and know it fast; there's no intervening curtain. It was an awkward assignment but it was the nearest I've got to being "on the road" in London. A Subterranean rush of emotion, taken direct with all the chance interruptions of an evening in someone else's house with another guest. I haven't indicated all the gaps on the tape; as many as 20 times we stopped the tape when the phone rang or Miles and his friends passed through. Then there is the background music, mostly Baroque by Corso's choice, which contributed greatly to the atmosphere. We disagreed not only about aspects of poetry but about the way in which the interview should be conducted: Corso wouldn't let me draw Miles's girlfriend into the conversation. Fair enough. Now a year after the event I have an eternal image of the gangster Neanderthal, born again in our time with classic Italian features, graying and bowed, but still shooting his body and thoughts across a beat café table. The romantic showman in an era grim with closed strivings and compromise; with all the dope and drink, with all the self-indulgence, this man's got a right to speak.

The story of those who have lived close to the edge, without recourse to a saving philosophy or religion, is chronicled vividly in Corso's work. The failures, the alienation of friends, are part of a life bursting beyond itself but pure – something the poet tries to explain in "Columbia U Poesy Reading –1975":

> "I'm not ashamed!" I screamed
> "You have butchered your spirit!" roared Ganesha
> "Your pen is bloodied!" cawed the scribe Thoth
> "You have failed to deliver the Message!" admonished
>   Hermes
> With tearful eyes I gazed into Her eyes and cried:
> "I swear to you there is in me yet time
> to run back through life and expiate
> all that's been sadly done … sadly neglected …"
>
> Seated on a cold park bench
> I heard Her moan: "O Gregorio, Gregorio
> you'll fail me, I know"
>
> Walking away
> a little old lady behind me
> was singing: "True! True!"
> "Not so!" rang the spirit, "Not so!"

This is not celebration or self-pity; it is a recognition of the artist's situation, particularly the fate of the beat writer that Kerouac portrays so often.

Corso decided to end the interview at what seemed like an arbitrary point. We went towards the restaurant but he wanted to stop at a pub on the way. We had a couple of drinks and I tentatively suggested that we should put a few more details on the tape to round things off; this, coming so soon after my comments about editing, caused Corso to demand that I hand over the cassette to him. Bluffing, I said, "You can have the thing anyway, it's no use to me." We had come close to blows. The barman was getting nervous and the fruit machines were not ready to deliver. Corso said he wasn't hungry and that we should go back to the house, which we did. Very little brandy remained. He gave me back the tape, gesturing that the evening was dead. I made my exit, slewed. God knows how I made it home. The next evening, at the Riverside, he put his arm round me and said, "I didn't want to let you drive after that, man. You should've stayed or something." All smiles and sweetness from the heart; another day is another day with all attendant changes.

The tape slept in my drawer for a while. After transcribing it I sent the manuscript across the ocean to be checked by the poet. Naturally, I wanted an accurate text. The package was returned: "Not deliverable as addressed. Unable to forward." It was an ironic twist. I wrote to Corso's editor at New Directions for confirmation of the address. I tried again with the postal code. The package was returned: "Attempted not known." Okay, Gregory, it fits somehow; you were always on the move. I just hope I've done you justice and no hard feelings, right?

THE INTERVIEW

SELERIE: I'd like you to tell me about your background in New York – the East Side.

CORSO: My background did not start with the East Side; it started with Greenwich Village, which is the West Side. I was born on Bleeker/McDougal Street which is the heart of Greenwich Village, which has a combination of Italian immigrants mixed with some of the sharpest heads all over the planet, who live there. Meaning the Bohemian types, the writers. Edna St. Vincent Millay lived there – or you name 'em – the writers who were part of that scene. And then, of course, the tourists which came down on the weekend, and they never see any of the people who live there, the residents; they only see each other and they point out to each other and say, "There's one." But all they do is come down with masquerade, try to act like they're Bohemian. This is as a kid that I saw it; remember now, this is before the beatniks and all that. Anyway, it was the hippest place in town and I thought, "A big city like New York – oh yeah. Tops." And as I grew up in it and the years changed there was moving around. I moved up over Lower East Side and I was adopted by eight foster parents, man, till I was about ten years old. My father took me back home, back to Greenwich Village, and he thought by taking me out of the orphanage he'd be out of the World War, too. But no way – they got him anyway. He went in the Navy and then I lived on the streets.

SELERIE: You lived on the streets?

CORSO: I had no father and no mother. My father went into the armed services and I never saw my mother – I don't know what happened to her. Nobody knows. Yeah, I have a belly button! Anyway, I lived on the streets and did pretty good until I got caught stealing, what was it? I kicked in a restaurant window, went in and took all the food that I wanted, and while coming out I was grabbed.

SELERIE: You were really hungry?

CORSO: Oh yeah. They put me in the Tombs. Now the Tombs, like the name says, are so horrible that they had to close it down. Today it doesn't exist and people go in the electric chair and all that. I was what? – twelve years old – and I was thrown in the cells with these people, so I learned fast.

SELERIE: Did other people in the cells teach you stuff?

CORSO: Not those, not that time. All they wanted to do was fuck and of course I saved my virginity by fighting back. The lucky thing was that I was Italian; when the other Italians saw me fight back, they came to my defence. If you don't fight back then they call you a "free-hole" – that was the expression. So I fought back; I saved my virginity. They let me out when I was 13. These were big war years, right? '43, 1943, and I'm out on the streets again. But this time I didn't have a place to sleep. So again I kick in a window and I go to sleep in this place, which was called the Educational Alliance; it was a place where the kids in the neighborhood go, like an alternative place. In those early days it was that – boy scouts, all kinds of things. And I fell asleep there. Police come in with the night watchman; they see me on the floor and they bring me right back to the Tombs thing again. I spent four months there in the hottest summer time – it was hell, man alive, and I really couldn't take it anymore and I got very sick in my body and they sent me to the hospital. Now the hospital was called Bellevue Hospital; it was where they put runaway boys but because it was 1943 they had no room for the boys and it was crowded, so all the mad people were there. I was put with those who were least mad but one day I rolled up a piece of white bread and I popped it in the air – a little ball – and it hit somebody's eye, who started screaming and pointing at me. And everybody started pointing at me. They grabbed me and put me in a straightjacket and threw me up to a room on the fourth floor where old women were screaming, where men were peeing in each other's mouths. The ball game was over, the whole thing was over already, and I was 13 years old when I caught that shit. Didn't even know about jerking off yet – total innocent – so I got the heavy thing fast. Get out of that one now. How old am I? – about 15 and a half; I'm out on the streets and I'm tough now. I make sure I'm gonna go after whatever the fuck is on that planet. So all I saw was just that.

SELERIE: Appetite, violence?

CORSO: No, to be smart. I used to go to the library all of the time and read the books as best I could – books on rhetoric, for instance. How do you get smart, Gregory? You see, I went to the sixth grade and that was the highest I ever went. How do you get smart? – you got to read books, but *what* books? I had no friends or anything to tell me this shit; I had to check it out myself. Rhetoric – I don't know where the fuck I heard that word but I thought that's what made you smart. Do you know how many books they have on rhetoric that were done about 1895 or the late 19th century? Thousands! – of this fucker on rhetoric. Then I thought, "What do I need with rhetoric?" I met this kid in the library when the war was over, and he had this great idea. He said, "Hey, you know these Army-Navy stores that are selling walkie-talkies? If we buy four of these things we can get a lot of money." I said, "How?" He said, "We gotta get two more guys; one drives a car and speaks through the walkie-talkie to the guy on the stairway, who relays to the guys breaking the safe that no cops are coming." That's putting crime on a scientific basis and that I ate up. I said, "Great, about time. Now if I'm going to that fucking jail again with all that horror, at least it's for something – not that shit of going up because I fell asleep or needed something to eat." This is a big one. Okay, so he has some money, this kid. His name is John but he never gave his last name. Dig the game. Picked up two other guys. What happens is we get 26 thousand dollars. Now this is 1945–6, so that's a lot of money. We shared the money and broke up. John goes off, I go off to Florida. I leave big tips, I buy zoot suits, like a real asshole, you know. The two Irish kids open up a bar mitzvah hall where people get married and all that kind of thing and buy hams, turkeys, bushels of whiskey and all this crap – invite the whole neighbourhood in. After a while the police get suspicious because here are these guys, 15, 16 years old, supplying everyone with drinks and food. Where'd they get all this money? They questioned the kids, who were drunk as hell, and they gave my name to the cops. The kids know my name, you see, though I don't know the other guy's name – thank god I never knew. When the police came and got me down in Florida they beat the shit out of me, saying, "What's John's last name?" I said, "I don't know," and that's why I was given the most time in prison – three years in Dannemora, Clinton Prison. The judge said I was a menace to society because I had put crime on a scientific basis. I did three years there – from the beginning of 17 years old to the end of 19; that's 1947–1950. I am so happy I never knew that guy's name 'cause once you mention the name of a partner in crime, mister, your life is over. If you squeal you blow it. I was lucky. I never got the fuckers who squealed on me but I didn't care; they were just kids anyway. So the first thing I learned was: "Never give your name to strangers while you're doing a crime." I took the lickings, went to prison, and that's where I learned, I think, the rest of that smell.

Three shots were laid on me in prison. First of all: "Don't take your shoes off" – which meant you're walking right out. Because three years was a cinch compared to the 36 years or a lifetime given to others. People go to the electric chair but I'd been given a different path. The next thing they said was: "Don't you serve time; let time serve you." That's when I got off rhetoric and ate up all the books. That's when I got into Stendhal, into Hugo, into Shelley, into all the goody-gumdrops. I ate up the 1905 *Standard Dictionary*, every word; it was about this thick (*gestures*). All the archaic and obsolete words – ate it up. So I didn't serve time, I let time serve me. I was fed well and because I was young I had a kind of mascot status. The last shot was given to me as I'm walking out of the prison. Big Mafioso man, who never spoke to me, gives me this hit: "When you're talking to two people when you're out there, make sure you see three." I thought, "What does this mean?" and I said, "Oh yeah, of course, *dig yourself*." That's where you get the control. If I'm talking to two people, make sure that I'm there too, and then everything's gonna be in harmony and fine. But if you're talking to two people and you don't know that you're there, you're out of control, man. It's a dangerous game in life. So the only thing I'm left with on that one was what about participation? What about getting happy-drunk sometimes and just let things abandon for a while. Well, that's happened to me in life and I've been in good fortune; I never got hurt when I was in abandon. I'm in my weakest moment when I'm in that state. Any fuckers want to get me, they can get me then, but you see I'm a very smart man, a happy one. I don't hurt nobody – nothing like that. When I let myself go in abandon, well yeah, if they want to get my arse they can do it.

SELERIE: What do you mean exactly by the phrase "in abandon"?

CORSO: When I let it all go, I don't give a fuck what happens. I just trust people and they sense everything's gonna be all right. They know who the fuck I am already, take it easy 'cause I don't hurt anybody. I don't expect to be hurt, so I'm not. That was the last shot they laid on me in prison – being when you talk to two, make sure you see three, same as if you talk to one, make sure you see two, and so on.

So that's the upbringing. Now, 20 years old, I come out and I go back to Greenwich Village. Now, of course, I'm a wealthy man.

SELERIE: With the stuff you got from the safe?

CORSO: It's all in my head. Not the money from the safe. No, that's not wealth; that I spent dumb, leaving big tips and buying zoot suits. Are you kidding? The money was not the game; it was what I *learned* and that's why I came out rich. Now, who did I meet right away with the richness is Allen Ginsberg, William Burroughs, Kerouac, all those fuckers. Because I was one of the rare people around that had the head.

SELERIE: Were they famous then or not?

CORSO: No, they only had good heads. They were smart.

SELERIE: Who struck you as having most artistic impulse in that group?

CORSO: I would say Kerouac for his sweetness, his gentility; there was no mean streak in him like I would find maybe sometimes in Ginsberg. That's why he [Ginsberg] has got to kill his ego all the time in these Buddhist schools; he's got something to kill, right? I used to joke with him and say, "Catch that man, he's killing his ego," or run after a guru and say, "That guru's killing my friend's ego." Whereas Kerouac was out of that shit already; he knew who he was and all that and he put his ego to good work. You know when it's energy, *spiritus*, you don't kill that shit if it's good; it's not hurting anybody. But Ginsie – he knew that in himself he had this hurt, pain with his mother when he was a kid or some shit. I don't know what it was – pain of all Jews maybe. Who knows?

SELERIE: Cain's curse.

CORSO: Whatever it is, that's what he's stuck with. So I didn't take up on him as much as I did with Kerouac. The other guy I dug a lot was Burroughs because he was a smart man already; he learned it through the druggie pool – the street scene of an old aristocratic kind of man.

SELERIE: Was he on heroin then?

CORSO: Yeah, at the time I met him. But, dig, he was like the people I knew in prison. I remember the people I knew in prison; I was very fortunate to know them – they came from 1910, 1920, 1930. I did not know the fuckers from 1940, 1950, 1960, 1970! I didn't know these dumb arses who are in jail today; I knew the smart babies who were … They're not *that* smart because they were in, but nonetheless it was a different kind of social rebellion in those days.

SELERIE: How was it different?

CORSO: First of all, they were not in there for drugs. They weren't in there for any kind of cornball thing that they would put people in jail for today. Burroughs was a *sharp* man. Remember these were friends; these are guys who were not known at that time. They were not the Burroughs, Ginsberg and Kerouac that you talk about.

SELERIE: You weren't conscious that this scene with its insights and excitement was going to be mythologized in the way it has been?

CORSO: I would say no, but maybe a guy like Ginsberg was aware of the heads that were around then, 'cause he was a man who knew where literature was going. He was a Columbia University student. Remember I would score hard knocks coming out of prison. So he might have known. Allen, you know, is no dummy.

SELERIE: When exactly did you start writing? You'd got all this stuff in your *head* then.

CORSO: Yeah. You remember when I told you I went to the library as a kid looking for rhetoric? Well, that would be the beginning. My first writing – pen to paper – was done in that same Astor Library on 42nd Street and 5th Avenue, the biggest library in New York City. And the feelings that I put out there were very funny. It was the first poem I ever wrote:

> My mother hates the sea,
> my sea especially,
> I warned her not to;

it was all I could do.
Two years later
the sea ate her.

It's called "Sea Chanty" and what that meant obviously was that my mother left me. I never saw her; she must have taken a boat back to Italy. It's the only way I can see that poem. That was the first shot. Now that was when I was about 15 or 16 years old, though I forgot about the poem and had to put it in a later book. My first book came out about 1954 – that would be eight years later, when I was 24. *Vestal Lady* was the title – yeah, you have it there. Dig this one:

Greenwich Village Suicide

Arms outstretched
hands flat against the windowsides
She looks down
Thinks of Bartok, Van Gogh
And New Yorker cartoons
She falls

They take her away with a Daily News on her face
And a storekeeper throws hot water on the sidewalk

See how cold that is? See this motherfucker? See how I saw?

SELERIE: Mean.

CORSO: Very, but that's what I saw. Now why did I put in her head "Bartok, Van Gogh / And New Yorker cartoons"? 'Cause it's *Greenwich Village* suicide. Those are the kind of people that live down there, other than the Italians who don't know shit from Bartok and Van Gogh. All right? Okay, that's early – baby Corso – this is maybe when I'm about 19.

SELERIE: *Vestal Lady* has a kind of animal closeness to experience. That poem you read has a mean vision but it says a lot about New York.

CORSO: Well, these people were mean to themselves. They committed suicide and I saw just what they did – that's all. Meanness on their part, not mine.

SELERIE: Did you get any recognition for that book?

CORSO: Umm, yeah. That's why *Gasoline* came out. When Ferlinghetti saw that book, *Vestal Lady*, he asked me to do this one – *Gasoline*.

SELERIE: *Vestal Lady* was privately printed or something – by subscription.

CORSO: Well, the girls at Radcliffe and the boys at Harvard got together, put up I think it was a thousand, six hundred bucks to come up with the book. And they got all their money back! They came out with a thousand copies and they were selling for a dollar apiece. But the copies that they kept are going out today for $150, signed ones for $200.

SELERIE: They kept some behind in their basement, I guess. Just let me ask you this – it's going forward in time. You came back to Harvard for some experiments with Leary didn't you?

CORSO: No.

SELERIE: You weren't in on that?

CORSO: I don't do experiments with the Leary types. Are you kidding? I was there at Harvard before Leary. I'm the man who gave him marijuana at Harvard.

SELERIE: Did you ever know Charles Olson?

CORSO: Yeah.

SELERIE: What do you remember about him?

CORSO: What's to tell about him? He died.

SELERIE: Was he a father figure?

CORSO: To me? No, I had no need of father figures and I'm not of that school.

SELERIE: I know you're not associated with Black Mountain but to a certain extent these labels are deceptive. I just wondered what you thought of him.

CORSO: I never dug him too much but I don't want to deprecate the dead.

SELERIE: Let's go into *Gasoline* now. That title seems to be fuel for the city mind. How does this work differ from *Vestal Lady* as a collection? Do you see some predominant change of direction here?

CORSO: There are some sharp little ones in the second book too, but suddenly I was getting to the biggies; I was hitting on the big fuckers. Let's see (*flicking through* Gasoline). This is a more major poem:

> Last night I drove a car
>> not knowing how to drive
>> not owning a car
> I drove and knocked down
>> people I loved
>> … went 120 through one town.
>
> I stopped at Hedgeville
>> and slept in the back seat
>> … excited about my new life.

See the change coming there? I become the monster man. I'm driving this fucking car, I'm knocking down people I love, and after I do that I go in the back seat and go to sleep "excited about my new life." (*Laughs uproariously*)

SELERIE: Sounds like a little violent angel.

CORSO: I know, of course. Loony terms. But that's when I woke up that people were nuts, that people go chop chop. For instance, I read in the paper in those times, this guy went to a movie theatre with an axe and people were watching this movie and I swear he held up this axe and went chop, chop, chop.

SELERIE: During a Bette Davis movie.

CORSO: I don't know what it was but it's weird. I mean, you imagine someone goes to a movie to relax and be nice, but this guy cuts through the romance.

SELERIE: Like those melancholics who hover on the sidelines in Shakespeare's plays.

(*Champagne is brought in.*)

CORSO: Happy birthday, babes!

SELERIE: Spontaneous poem on Champagne opening for Miles's birthday!

CORSO: We'll give a shot to her [Miles's girlfriend]. May you get all that's not coming to you. That's an awful lot!

SELERIE: Shelley was an influence on your writing by this time, I suppose.

CORSO: He was a smart fucker. He was a revolutionary of the spirit. He's the one who said, "Die if you want to be with that which you seek" – forget it already. If you want that, then drop dead, go ahead and die.

SELERIE: And you thought that was pretty appropriate to the times?

CORSO: Oh sure – to any time. Can you imagine these motherfuckers who want to find out what life's about and they knocked themselves out all their lives trying to figure it out. Did you ever meet those kind of people? Do you ever want to know what this life's about, man? (*Laughs*)

SELERIE: That could be "amputating the rose" in order to know it, as you said somewhere. But maybe you mean ...

CORSO: No. You get a guy like Hitler who undertook the death of whole world. Watch out!

SELERIE: Can poetry be instrumental in combating fascism?

CORSO: Yeah. Knock him out.

SELERIE: With words?

CORSO: No. Figurative niceness! Poets are still alive, he's dead. I was told to look out for the National Front and when I was in Brighton I saw about 19 of these young fuckers on the train station. I went right up to them and I said "Hi."

SELERIE: They probably thought you were an ex-Hell's Angel.

CORSO: Okay, they may have thought that, but I said, "Hey, you know, this Hitler guy fascinates me too." I wonder about him that he could get so many people under his egosis – that power that he exercised, you know. So one of them said, "Hey, what shall we do with this one?" But one of the elders came out from the group and defended me. He said, "What the man said is correct."

SELERIE: That you need to get into that consciousness to understand it?

CORSO: Yeah. What I said was, "This man is a fascinating man and you should check him out." But these guys fell for him; those assholes fall for him like they fall for God or Jesus. Look at Bob Dylan. (*To Miles*) See this – your mother's poem. I wrote underneath it to your father: "Hey, Jay, dig what your wife wrote that I wrote at the same time."

SELERIE: About him joining "the oldest roadshow on earth?"

CORSO: Bob Dylan, he an old showman,
        himself joined the oldest roadshow on earth.

MILES: You get those National Front guys – the skinheads – before a group goes on. I mean with a group who they actually like. They go on and they say, "Sieg Heil!" at a gig. Now, as a musician, I'd be upset if someone did that to me. You're a poet – what would happen if someone …

CORSO: How can they handle their ashes afterwards? Go ahead, do this "Sieg Heil" shot. What are they going to do afterwards? You're up there, a single spirit making your music. They gotta be grouped. The fucker won't do it alone; he's got to do it with a whole bunch of guys.

SELERIE: So you need to get into the spirit of fascism to understand it?

CORSO: No, I was just amazed to see it here and figure England, you know, could be tougher than Germany. Because people are a little afraid to come out like that there. They did and they lost. But England if they play the game …

MILES: When punk started …

SELERIE: When people get really ground down in economic terms they start looking for scapegoats.

CORSO: But punk did a great thing with it. Punk tried to knock it out by taking their symbols. That's a different story.

SELERIE: This reminds me of your poem "Bomb," in which you enter into the consciousness of the weapon, seeking to understand it, rather than retreating in absolute fear.

CORSO: Now you got it.

SELERIE: Ferlinghetti did that as a broadside, didn't he?

CORSO: Yeah, and it's in *Happy Birthday of Death*, which comes after *Gasoline*.

SELERIE: That poem and "Marriage" seem to be the big statements from around that time.

CORSO: A lot of people like "Marriage" – I made a lot of money on that poem. It's the only one where you could talk about money. I made over $10,000 through the years. Can you imagine?

SELERIE: There's a beautiful version of that on one of the John Giorno records. It's like a five minute play, a little piece slicing up the American dream. The scenes are like something overheard in a bar.

CORSO: But these are not oral poems; there's art there. I made myself a poet – it's a high class business.

SELERIE: Sure, I realize that this is something more ordered than random conversation. But you keep the experience "live."

(*Break in tape. Music in background. Corso conducting "ya-da-da-da" while conversation goes on.*)

CORSO: This is Lully. He ran the French court under Louis Quatorze, the Sun King.

SELERIE: Were you listening to this kind of music in the early days?

CORSO: Yeah. 1954 this shot I heard first.

SELERIE: So you were into this more than you were into, say, jazz?

CORSO: Well, why say "more than"? I was listening to Berlioz and Verdi in 1950. I was listening to Miles Davis in '54.

SELERIE: Why do you have a galactic picture on the cover of *Long Live Man*?

CORSO: That's my sperm. You see, it looks like the Crab Nebula. I shot and put it in these two pieces of glass. You put it under a microscope – the guy had the camera for it at Mount Palomar and he took it there. They've got a tremendous telescope but they do it reverse and the shot was taken, dig it now, from the macro to the micro. That's my come; that's why I said, "Long Live Man." Now this is before Women's Lib. Dig the ball game: when you use the word "Man" it entails everybody, but today you gotta be careful. After Women's Lib, I have to put two more vowels with it – "Humankind." I can't say "Mankind," I can't say "Man," I gotta say "Humankind."

SELERIE: Does that sound awkward? You'd have to lengthen the lines in that first poem in the book.

CORSO: With some rhythmical things it works, but the "Man" shot is fast: "Hey, man, are you kidding?" – it's a big baby. "Baby," right? Neuter. "Man" is neuter in that kind of expression in language. What's the species called? "Homo sapiens," right? What's "Homo" mean?

SELERIE: Man.

CORSO: Right.

SELERIE: A generic term.

CORSO: It ain't my fault folks! (*Laughs*) No, I learned after that I don't use "Man" anymore in my poetry. I use "Humankind." I make sure 'cause I love women, man, I love 'em. I say, "Sure, man, if they've been held down by that shit, better change it. Change the ball game."

SELERIE: Are there many female writers you admire? What about Diane di Prima?

CORSO: No, she's a very smart woman but she doesn't say anything for me. I like Sappho – tough shot! Emily D. I would say that's about it. Maybe Jean Rhys.

SELERIE: Are you hopeful that there's a lot of good writing to come, now women are playing a fuller role in society?

CORSO: I'm hopeful that people can sing. Sure, women are past our fucking accolades.

SELERIE: You say here [on the back cover of *The Happy Birthday of Death*]:

> How I love to probe life. That's what poetry is to me, a wondrous prober ... It's not the metre or measure of a line, a breath; not "law" music; but the assembly of great eye sounds placed into an inspired measured idea.

How does that relate to Dylan Thomas's idea that poetry begins "with the substance of words" rather than a clear pattern of thought? Would you say that the linking of sounds is what produces meaning or vice versa?

CORSO: It's just the way you look at it. If you look at the words "Ionic," "Corinthian," "Cyprus," "Supplicant," "Doric" – these are the "i" sounds – so beautiful.

SELERIE: So when you're writing you just listen for the music? You wait for it to come and it comes?

CORSO: My music is built in – it's already natural. I don't play with the metre. It's a built-in shot, right? Now the big thing I've got to do with the poetry is this: I've got to have it short and fast; so it's the "measured idea." In other words, you're not writing a novel, you're not writing a fucking vignette; what you're doing is a poem and that means four fucking lines maybe or one line which is verse. Like, what is verse? One line or the whole game? The whole epic or one line is called verse. Verse can be one line, right?

SELERIE: Shorter than haiku.

CORSO: Oh, but the couplet is before the haiku. I do use recognizable forms like the sonnet but …

SELERIE: You don't start off with the intention of writing a sonnet and then look for a subject.

CORSO: Well, you have a sense of how it might be because you've used certain forms before. But you don't hold the baby down; you let the poem happen.

SELERIE: We've only talked about the early books so far.

CORSO: Here's the process: *Vestal Lady, Gasoline, Happy Birthday, Long Live Man, Elegiac Feelings American,* and then the book that's coming out, *Heirlooms.*

SELERIE: There's an air of high culture about that last title.

CORSO: That's it. It's the golden dot I put in my poetry babes. See, there are two books missing in all this. They were lost. One was stolen and that book was called *Who am I – Who I am.*

SELERIE: How did that get stolen?

CORSO: They knew it was a good fucking book – in 1974. It was in two suitcases and I had all my letters from Kerouac and everything and I was living in this fucking Chelsea Hotel in New York City. A supposed friend, a woman, who's a very rich lady and all this shit, a poet named Isabella Gardner,[4] got hold of it; once it was in her hands, it was gone.

SELERIE: What did she do with it?

CORSO: Well, she was very jealous of me, you see, 'cause there again … Remember I gave you my background – prison guy, schoolkid, and yet I was having the ball game with the poetry. I was really collecting, I was making it, I was writing the goodies and she knew that that was my book. So there was a big gap – 1970–1974 – four years' work, gone. I got so fucking pissed at that shit, man, I said, "*Forget* it" for two years. That led up to 1976 and I said, "Hey, wait a minute. The poet's not gone. They can fuck my poetry around but they didn't fuck the poet around." And that's from *Heirlooms*, which is the work I'm reading lately to people – the new poems.

SELERIE: Do you know what happened to those other poems?

CORSO: Destroyed or stolen or hidden.

SELERIE: Do you think someone's sitting on them?

CORSO: Sure. She doesn't need money so she ain't selling.

SELERIE: They might be in the bowels of some library.

CORSO: No.

SELERIE: Archives. Remember what happened to *The Waste Land* manuscript.

CORSO: No. They could be burnt or they could be held by this person, or somebody could have taken the material from her – somebody who knew the value of it. Even if my manuscripts didn't mean shit, it was the letters that I got from my friends like Kerouac, who had died, let's see, six years beforehand. I had all his letters – letters from Burroughs and Kerouac. All of my suitcases, all my valuables, I carried a round with me, 'cause I moved around a lot.

SELERIE: The man with his house on his head.

CORSO: Whatever you're gonna do. The janitor would sell off. But still I said, "Fuck it, they didn't get the poet and there's more where that came from."

SELERIE: You tend to have long intervals between publishing books.

CORSO: I told you – the losses, they're stolen.

SELERIE: That explains all?

CORSO: Yes.

SELERIE: What happened to that little poem which appeared in *New*

Departures? Something like "Truth is Eternity / Sojourning / In Time."

CORSO: "Sojourning / In Time" – yes.

SELERIE: That reminds me of some of Kerouac's stuff in *Mexico City Blues*.

CORSO: Whatever – I don't care whatever it came out of. That was part of the stuff that was lost. That one was saved but it's just one little line.

SELERIE: I love that – I could write it on my bathroom wall.

CORSO: Well, anyway, that was saved – only because it was published in a little magazine.

SELERIE: Okay. Let's go back to *Elegiac Feelings American*. How is that different from *The Happy Birthday of Death*?

CORSO: Well, it differs in this way. This book was put together. All the poems in here were done very early but they all had to do with death – the death of the American Indians, the death of their god, the death of Jack Kerouac, the death of Kennedy. When Kerouac died I said, "Okay, they can put a book out." See, I would never put this one out. *Who am I – Who I am* was the book to come out – the big one – and that was fucked and taken. So I said, "All right, put this one out. If they want it here it is." If Kerouac didn't die this book would never have been out. No way – because it doesn't make any sense otherwise. It's all elegies.

SELERIE: Kerouac's death caused you to meditate on that theme?

CORSO: But this book was written through the years. I don't write these poems all on one day about death.

SELERIE: Right. So you collected them.

CORSO: I would not have bothered to collect them if Kerouac hadn't died. The *Heirlooms* gives me one great thing. When asked the question, "Who am I?" I answered, "Who I am." That learning is never lost – that's why it's called *Heirlooms* and that's where I put the golden dot. So it might be all for the good that that poetry went, because this stuff now is more chiseled – it's like a big brick musehouse [or a shithouse, which means solid]. The golden dot – it's the end. So I came to this country and put the relay to it, in a reading of the obvious. Now I give it to you back England. America's handled your language – fine fucking language too, it's kept the English language vital, and now I say, "I give it back to you."

SELERIE: Just as the word "faucet," which existed in Shakespeare's time, has been lost over here but is being sent back via American literature and films.

CORSO: But the Americans lost so much …

SELERIE: You've got it back by living on the street and getting that raw power into literature. Marlowe had some of that urgency in Elizabethan times.

CORSO: I'm the man that's handing it back – and not through living on the street. I'm not the one who lived on the street.

SELERIE: I wasn't suggesting you were a bum!

CORSO: Whether you lived on the street or in an ivory tower, it don't mean no shit. It's who you are to know this game. Who am I to bring the fucking torch back here? I give it back to England for the simple reason that the poets that were or tried to be – the would-be's, Bob Dylan and all that – fell for these gods. To do that means they no longer themselves can say anything to lead, to illuminate, the heads of people.

SELERIE: Because they bow down before some unchangeable higher presence.

CORSO: God – and Love – hurt so many people. Anybody that kowtows can never write a poem for *you*; in other words, they can never illuminate you.

SELERIE: Because it's blind faith.

CORSO: Whatever the fuck it is, they kowtow. So I'm not the kowtower. I say, Babe, before it all goes – because I'm a physical shot, right? – bring the relay back and tell England: "Look, maybe it won't happen in your country but it's certainly going to happen with the English language. It's gonna be taken away from the United States already. The States has fucked up an awful lot in the last 15 years, man."

SELERIE: But the capitalist/imperialist dream has provoked some extraordinary reaction from people who were opposed to the establishment line. Think of the anti-war movement in the Sixties. Even Watergate must have brought out an increased awareness of the way things work in government ...

CORSO: They all do, they all bring out. Anybody that's in a state of power brings out. Remember America became beautiful with the language at Eisenhower's time. That's because the country really hit well – they weren't yet doing too much of dirty numbers. The dirty number was still from Hitler and Stalin. But then America got into the dirty act and once they do that they lose their poetry. When a country is up there they get the best poetry; like England was at the height of its power when you had Shelley, Keats and Wordsworth. That's when the English get their power with the poetry. America's fallen – that's why I said, "Elegiac Feelings American." Allen Ginsberg called his book *The Fall of America*. *Elegiac Feelings American* is a little cooler because the feelings that I had were more ... Well, if you say the "fall" of something then you have to be really definite with that shot. I pass the English language around. See that eye? He knew what the fuck he was talking about. Now I didn't say when I read this at the Abbey, "England where are your poets?" to be answered by prophecy. But you better watch. In the years to come you'll see that the English language is not just going to be American. England went to the golden calf for I don't know how long with their rock and roll – they gave up poetry.

SELERIE: Do you really think that's the golden calf?

CORSO: Sure.

SELERIE: It could be a return to animal energy, more elemental rhythms.

CORSO: But where's the English poetry?

SELERIE: Some people, I think, have derived a spontaneity of expression from rock music, though perhaps jazz had a more important influence on our poets. Actually, Allen Ginsberg thinks that Mick Jagger is a poet, as far as his phrasing and movement are concerned.

CORSO: That's great – when they went to their golden calf you better believe it was gold. The Beatles, the Rolling Stones – top class but that's where it is, that's all; they're not poets.

SELERIE: Just a lower level of communication?

CORSO: Not lower, not higher, just different. Poets sing in another way. But the word, like I say, will go back to Angleterre. You say you're an expert on Shakespeare …

SELERIE: Well, I studied his work for a long time. It's a measure of what is possible in language.

CORSO: Watch the ball game. "Fat as butter … cheap as an egg." Two greatest lines Shakespeare ever wrote. Where's that from?

SELERIE: *Henry IV.* I can't place it exactly.

CORSO: You should know your subject. Anyway, you can see there's something special in those lines.

(Gap in tape)

SELERIE: "Don't you understand how nice it is?" you said. What do you mean?

CORSO: Well that you can see these things going down before you, right? You can see it happening and you see the changes. The Beatles, the Rolling Stones, they ain't no more; they were, and whatever's held in the archives of them will be so played, but rarer and rarer. Whereas the poetry is always held. When I publish this book, *Vestal Lady*, in 1954, you look at the best seller list of the time and you see that the novels of that time aren't even known today, whereas this still gets published because the poems are taught in colleges and high schools. So the poetry keeps on being reprinted, both in the original volumes and in anthologies. Whereas those other pieces of shit that got all these people millions of dollars came and went. *(Chuckles)* So what's the real word? Not the entertainment one. The entertainment word comes from those people who have the best sellers and that's their celebrity; they buy it and they pay; they get a lot of money but they gotta pay for their celebrity. They're luckier than, say, the Hollywoodians, who are known for their faces and cannot have any privacy. You get a Marlene Dietrich very old and there's something scary about it; she feels abashed about it. They get a Marilyn Monroe that does herself in because of the painful changes – the exposure.

SELERIE: But Garbo managed to keep it together. She cut off.

CORSO: Whatever. She was wiser and she knew it at the time – to say that my life is separate and I'm not gonna be destroyed.

SELERIE: She was a shrewd lady. She fended off the probers while still keeping her fame.

CORSO: Sure but that's rare. So the pain mainly comes to those people. Now you get a novelist who's only known as a name; he'll get millions of dollars for writing that garbage, he doesn't suffer too much from publicity, but in the end he disappears. I mean people forget about the writer and the work.

SELERIE: Do you count Mailer in there or not?

CORSO: Well, Mailer continues. He goes on and on but I don't think anything that he wrote will remain. No, it's a bunch of shit, too.

SELERIE: So you're talking about all of these popular novelists. Bellow?

CORSO: No, they are – what are they called?

SELERIE: Ephemeral?

CORSO: No, not ephemeral. They are called the illustrious obscure.

SELERIE: There are English novelists like that too, I guess.

CORSO: Well, some stand out. Who's your last one? Fielding I like. Europeans – oh, Céline, now you're talking about great books. Old Ferdinand will remain. Mr. Burroughs will remain. Mr. Kerouac will remain.

SELERIE: No one else?

CORSO: Joyce.

SELERIE: Virginia Woolf?

CORSO: Remain.

SELERIE: Have you read John Berger's retelling of the Don Juan story?

CORSO: Oh, you mean the guy who writes *The Little Big Man*?[5]

SELERIE: No that's a different guy. Let me recommend the British novelist to you. His big novel is Q, plain Q like Thomas Pynchon's V. I think you would find that book interesting, more on a par with poetry in commitment and intensity.

CORSO: Well, I could recommend Flann O'Brien's work. Have you read *At Swim-Two-Birds* or *The Third Policeman*? I think he's very underrated; he's a top shot man – he'll survive.

SELERIE: Okay, so what is it in these people that makes them survive? Poetry?

CORSO: Not exactly. It's too easy to say, "Poetry is everything" like I usually do. What makes them survive? People's choice, I guess.

SELERIE: It must be some magical way of catching the essence of life, some weird way of making people say "that's it" or "that's what fascinates me." It's more than most people experience, yet recognizable as life.

CORSO: I don't know. This belief in magic …

SELERIE: It's not just entertainment, unless one includes some large element of disturbance in one's definition of that word.

CORSO: They say if you believe in magic somebody can spook you out; because you believe it, they've got you. I, a man who's in the middle, would never deny magic but I would never fall for it either, because I'm the wise man. If I denied it I'd be a dumb ass. Like, I don't deny the Bible. I'll deny nothing, man. I'll check out anything these human beings put on this planet.

I'll check it out but I won't fall for one – that's the kowtowing again. If you fall for one of those fuckers you kowtow. And don't you know that usually they have a book? Look at the Christians. They have the old book, the Old Testament.

SELERIE: Just as the Moslems have the Koran.

CORSO: Hallelujah, you got it!

SELERIE: That's the dangerous side of magic – to bow down before the one text. You mustn't have one way only.

CORSO: Oh, I don't say "mustn't." Spare me! I'm not the one who tells people how to live their lives. Me, I don't reject text; I'll eat up all their books.

SELERIE: Chew them! (*Laughs*)

CORSO: You better believe it – I take the essence and keep it in my head. Like I say, I don't have disrespect for it, nor do I have respect exactly. I don't owe respect. See, a lot of people want respect, man; people that have lots of money want respect. Now, why should I respect them for their fucking money? – people that wrote some piece of shit and got a lot of money for it. I don't owe them respect but also I'm not disrespectful – that's what matters. I'm spared them. The motherfuckers can't touch me 'cause I'm not being disrespectful. But, boy oh boy, I'd be kowtowing if I gave them the respect that they wanted. Fuck them, man. I don't owe them nothing – it's true. These are the ones that are living off the fat of the mind, the ones that do your novels and are gonna earn all those millions of dollars.

SELERIE: You aren't drinking that stuff. Is it really bad?

CORSO: No man, I've got a taste for good fuckin' brandy – French shit. (*Laughs*) If I'm gonna drink, I'm gonna drink the good shit, that's all. I bought today – what do you call it? – a cigarette lighter. There's a dearth of matches in London because they do not give you matches with the cigarettes. I can't stand it – it drives me nuts because, you know, I'm a compulsive smoker and so I need my matches too. In prison, which is weird – now, I don't know if you have it in England 'cause you got these wooden matches – but in prison in America, where you have paper matches, if a guy has a pack of cigarettes and no matches, you can get a cigarette from him for a light. Now dig the ball game. If you're smoking a cigarette that's lit you pass it on; you get the cigarette. But if he wants a match to light up for later this is how you do it: you cut it in half, you open it up in the centre – boop, you got two matches 'cause each side has got the phosphorus. For that one shot that he holds for later you get two cigarettes. Now, if they want to save cigarettes in prison, this is what they do: "Can I have a cigarette? I haven't opened my pack yet." Sure they have, but on the bottom. They show you the top that is not open. Now that don't mean shit that they haven't opened their pack yet but you take it, you see. "Hey man, I haven't opened my pack yet." It's awful man, I'm telling ya, but the addictions of certain things and how people play the game.

SELERIE: You've certainly ranged through a lot of scenes – gone to the top and bottom. Do you feel you've lived beyond time?

CORSO: I'm going to give you two hits of how I turn time around. When I caught the fucker it was a human choice of a dimension. Time, yeah, I tumbled that very early in the game. Two short poems: one is called "The Last Gangster" and the other is called "Birthplace Revisited."

> I stand in the dark light in the dark street
> and look up at my window, I was born there.
> The lights are on; other people are moving about.
> I am with raincoat; cigarette in mouth,
> hat over eye, hand on gat.
> I cross the street and enter the building.
> The garbage cans haven't stopped smelling.
> I walk up the first flight; Dirty Ears
> aims a knife at me ...
> I pump him full of lost watches.

What I mean by that little turn at the end, see, it's almost sadistic or surrealistic to tell but I thought I could change the whole poem through the last line.

The Last Gangster

> Waiting by the window
> my feet enwrapped with the dead bootleggers of Chicago
> I am the gangster, safe, at last,

waiting by a bullet-proof window.

> I look down the street and know
> the two torpedoes from St. Louis.
> I've watched them grow old
> … guns rusting in their arthritic hands.

Yeah, I killed the fuckers – see, they had their guns ready for me. What a magic poetry is! The closest I could ever get to really writing a poem is this one – I must have been about 22 years old – to get the idea, try to sound like a poet. It's called "Amnesia in Memphis." I tried a big shot.

SELERIE: Yeah, I was thinking of how your poetry stretches across space and time. Another thing I like is your personification of Death, Beauty and Truth, as in the poem you read the other night.

CORSO: "The Whole Mess … Almost." I love doing that one with people.

SELERIE: There's a really wide sweep there but you, the individual, are in the centre of the scene. So it's not some T.S. Eliot-like retreat into detachment. You've got grime and shit with the angels in there too.

CORSO: When you think about it, shit does mulch and regenerate – it's all right.

SELERIE: Peter Orlovsky read an extraordinary poem about a woman with leprosy at the Round House last year. The horror was mixed with some deeper sense of a cycle of growth and decay. It's an attitude beyond western dualism, I suppose.

CORSO: Yeah, I saw that in his poetry. I wrote a preface for his book, you know.

SELERIE: What did you think of that Westminster Abbey reading? Really, honestly.

CORSO: Well, firstly, let's get this straight: when you say "honestly" what do you think I'm going to say? Why use that cliché?

SELERIE: It's a British response meaning "cut beneath ..."

CORSO: Like when people say "take care," meaning they're really wishing you well. But I've been taking care of myself for 50 fucking years. So ...

SELERIE: I admit we're wrapped up in all kinds of politeness; we aren't direct in our behaviour.

CORSO: It's not politeness there, it's using cliché. You said "honestly." All right, the reason I'm picking on that is this: who are these fucking poets to presume to say that they're going to give you the truth? What are they going to do? If they're not, are they going to give you a lie? You see what I mean? See, that's why I downed Truth early in the game. I said, "Bullshit, I'm not falling for that game." Dig it, if you've got the natural thing to say, that's all there is. You don't say, "Well now folks, I'm going to be truthful with you." I mean, big deal!

SELERIE: I thought that you were a real performer – not an entertainer but a performer.

CORSO: What did you think? Was I performing all right?

SELERIE: I liked "Neanderthal Man" in particular.

CORSO: I cared about something, right? And it made sense.

SELERIE: You were political in the best sense of the word. You weren't following a dogma, you weren't talking about remote ideas; you were talking about what *is* – now. And you weren't offering simple solutions. Take that one poem, "In Praise of Neanderthal Man" – your rehabilitation of the "bowlegged toiler" has implications for the gun-toting TV society of today. It puts things in perspective.

CORSO: – so again unto you I say O bigot anthropology
                  deem not Sir Neanderthal a stupid thing

See, you don't deny life, man. At his time, the Neanderthal was the "philosoph supreme." Remember, I didn't say, "philosopher." I showed him my class. That's poetry. If you say "philosopher supreme" it ...

SELERIE: Provides the wrong connotation.

CORSO: (*With emphasis*) "Philosoph supreme!" The fucking Neanderthal at his time was the top daddy – smartest head around. Then I have this poem "Metaphor" where I'm thinking of human beings whose days are running out and they're gonna wake up to that fact. The dinosaur ran out, so human beings'll run out. They're going to do it because their heads are very sharp and they'll burn themselves away. Then better things come along. So that's why I say, "Ay unto this Simeons and their new kind shall surely testify." I'll be around. The rest don't want to die, man; they say, "wowee."

SELERIE: It's funny that you said you weren't interested in Olson because he in fact was very respectful of that primitive life. He wanted to overturn the Greek assumption that older, less rational forms of life were inferior.

CORSO: Oh sure. I liked that in him. I like anybody who can sing and make sense – great!

SELERIE: D.H. Lawrence too?

CORSO: Same way. I like them all. But the Olson thing – I didn't have time. In other words, Olson was a daddy type to lots of people in poetry.

SELERIE: He wanted to hold the centre of the stage.

CORSO: Right. I told you again, I don't owe respect to nobody 'cause all I learned I learned on my ownsome. Although I did learn from humankind, it was I myself and humankind; ergo I have added to it. I take my stand as an individual within humankind, that's all. I don't quarrel with those ideas in Olson – the man had a very good head.

SELERIE: Did you go to visit him in Gloucester?

CORSO: No. I'm sorry. The only one I went to visit in my life was Auden. W.H. Auden.

SELERIE: Really?

CORSO: He wanted to read to me *The Tempest*. He knew that was my favourite

Shakespeare play so he said, "I'll read it to you."

SELERIE: Where was that?

CORSO: New York City. St. Mark's Place.

SELERIE: An apartment?

CORSO: Yeah. What year was that? 1964.

SELERIE: He read you parts of the play or the whole play?

CORSO: The whole shot.

SELERIE: The whole play – Jesus!

CORSO: We were drinking all afternoon and he loved it. You see, he loved me as a poet, though he was in a very different world with me and he knew it.

SELERIE: His was a gay world – clipped sophistication?

CORSO: Well, he knew I was the goods and that there was nothing at all that we really had to say. He was meeting his peer – the poet man, although I was much younger. It was the only way it could work out – we both knew that. I said, "Sure, I'll hear from the elder 'cause I dig his poetry." So I went to see him. He read me *The Tempest* and I got the goodies. That's his favourite play, too. Then we agreed on what the best play of all ever was: Euripides' *Bacchae*. The only argument we had was over Shelley. I said Shelley was the tough class fucking poet, but he didn't dig Shelley because he thought Shelley was the whole ... He took Shelley wrong.

SELERIE: Too much froth?

CORSO: He figured that Shelley was – when Shelley said, "woe is me," he said, "oh, woe is me" (*effete, effeminate voice*), whereas I told him Shelley said, "Oh! woe is me" (*bold, vigorous tone, wrathful even*).

SELERIE: There's this big misconception about Shelley, isn't there? People think he was some wayward dreamer who was all air and had no earthly concerns. Whereas, if you read a work like *Prometheus Unbound* or look at the facts of his life, a very concrete vision becomes evident. His poetry is intimately bound up with the political and social issues of that time. There's even the suggestion that knowledge of phenomena such as electricity can bring release from boring labour.

CORSO: But that a man like Auden could have this misconception amazed me. That's when I toppled him.

SELERIE: Many people over here still hold Auden's view, perhaps because of a certain hostility towards Shelley in departments of English Literature. That idea of him as a remote, self-indulgent figure is very prevalent; I suppose it's a way of avoiding the political impact of his work. He's presented as someone who was up in the skies, lost, wet ...

CORSO: (*Laughs*) Who do you think saved Shelley when he'd been lost for years? You're looking at the man right here. I'm the man who brought Shelley back. I gave it to Ginsberg – you better believe it – he woke up to who the fuck Shelley was. See, 'cause Shelley was a revolutionary of the spirit and that's big. When I was walking round Westminster Abbey with the Dean that day we looked over at the two old rare Ben Jonsons and I said, "Jeez, why do they have that redundancy here?" He said, "No, I want to hear what you said about Shelley before." I said, "Oh yeah. I want to know why you've got Shelley's name up there because he was an atheist." He says, "Well, you know, they finally understood in England that it made no matter what their beliefs were, this was one great poet." I said, "Well, hallelujah." And that's when I told him – I said, "You know what Shelley is to me?" He said, "What?" I said, "He was the first revolutionary of the spirit." He said, "That's a unique way of looking at it," and that's all. So, when he got up to introduce the poets, hear what he says: "Shelley – 'Poets are the unacknowledged legislators of the world.'" Right? This is what the Dean said. He mentioned Shelley.

SELERIE: He knew about it or do you think he looked it up after you spoke together?

CORSO: He knew – and that's why he dug me. 'Cause I said, "I want to know about Percy up there." I didn't know that Percy in English means "cock." (*Laughs*)

SELERIE: I suppose you relate to Shelley particularly because of his associations with Italy. He lived there a long time – about four years, I think.

CORSO: Yeah – "Leghorn" [Livorno].

SELERIE: I think it was very important to his vision that he went out there then. The French Revolution had failed and Napoleon had come and gone but there was still a sense of how society could change for the better. In *Prometheus Unbound* the Promethean fire seems Latin in inspiration. Maybe I'm just saying that his mythology and his poetry aren't insular.

CORSO: He went to free the Irish – in a little rowboat. People laughed at him but he knew what was happening there.

SELERIE: Going back to the Westminster Abbey reading, I thought you were the only person who was grounded – you had the beauty and you had the anger. John Cooper Clarke only had the urban sharpness; he didn't have the beauty. Michael Horovitz was off on some other planet reading other people's stuff and Frances [Horovitz] was BBC, you know. You were the only person who had both those things.

CORSO: What is both? "Both" is humour – a sense of humour. Remember? In that poem I mentioned that I had all the big subjects that poets write about in this room and I threw them out of the window – all of them.

SELERIE: That's like a Zen thing – to throw them out of the window.

CORSO: I threw them all out the window. But when I threw Beauty out I said, "You served me best in life," and I ran downstairs and caught her just in time and put her down. She said, "Oh, you saved me." I told her, "Yeah, but now move on," and I went back up to the room. See, in my head, I did right by that. You don't smash Beauty because Beauty's been nice to me in my life. I'm the poet man and Beauty served that well. Truth did not serve it well; Truth, I found out, is always a bulwark – it stopped me from going ahead. You say, "This is true," and you stop there, see? So I had no respect for Truth.

SELERIE: That's why you react against Christianity and all those fake …

CORSO: Well, I don't have to react against Christianity. I tell you, all those fakes I know them. You can ask me anything about Christianity. All the religions I know, 'cause it's my little satchel – poetry – got to know these things. I don't fall for it, that's all. A little bit of knowledge and a whole lot of faith and it leaves me very much alone in the world, Gavin. It can lead me where people like; people who I know like Dylan and Ginsberg all got their gods, even if Ginsberg's god is a no-god, the Buddhistic one. It leaves me alone. I say, "Gee whiz, man, even my close head friends – not my father who believes in Christ and all – but even my close head friends believe in it."

SELERIE: It's a cop-out?

CORSO: Not as a cop-out but there's something that leaves me very much alone. Ye gods! It's all spooky – I can't cop out.

SELERIE: Yours is a sane Shelleyan attitude – knowing Beauty and Death but not stopping. Like Shelley never … He did these scientific experiments in Oxford, didn't he? And got expelled for it. He wanted to discover for himself what made things tick, not accept received opinion.

CORSO: He got expelled for the atheism thing – *The Necessity of Atheism*. He did the scientific experiments in his little cottage and he blew it up all the time. Look at Rimbaud. Rimbaud vowed that he would never do like Baudelaire, his hero, did and go back to the church. Now Baudelaire, of course, when he broke with the church wrote about this great thrice magician; he wrote about the devil and got into magic and all that, but towards the end he got scared and ran back to the Catholic Church. Okay. Rimbaud vowed he would not do the same thing. The one leg went and then the other leg went; his sister comes in and says, "Believe in God. You're dying. Go to Christ." And he says, "Jesse, you're my sister. If you my sister believe then I should believe too." When he wasn't strong any more, when they got him at his weakest, he went back to the church.

SELERIE: People tend to fall back on what is definite. Dylan, having lost Sarah, was catapulted back …

CORSO: I don't put Bob Dylan in the same class as Rimbaud. Come on, man.

SELERIE: No, but there's the parallel movement – what happens to a person when they're weak or lost.

CORSO: What I mention about Dylan is only that he was an influence to people in his time. But I don't think Dylan will ever hit as many people as Rimbaud will.

SELERIE: I don't know about numbers but I agree that Rimbaud's art is of another order. Can we go back to Auden? What do you think of his regular use of accepted forms? How does that structure hit you?

CORSO: Can you realize that this has been going on a long time? How much longer do you want to go?

SELERIE: I said we'd go down to Uppers about 10 o'clock. It's only five minutes' walk from here. I'd like to go on if you don't mind because I've got one or two important questions left. We may have to cut some of the intermediate stuff – I don't know how much material we really have here.

CORSO: Oh yeah? You just made a big mistake. What in this world has to be cut? Leave it alone. You wanna talk to me, don't touch my arm.

SELERIE: You will have the decision about what's cut and what's left in.

CORSO: Decision for what?

SELERIE: I was just thinking of the people coming in and out, the talk about cigarettes, drink … me bringing you the wrong brandy. Okay, I won't cut anything. If you say "Don't cut," I won't cut.

CORSO: Course not, man, 'cause if you cut you're gonna have to then play with what I'm saying and it'll be so out of context, man. Don't you see, if you knock out a certain segment …

SELERIE: Okay. I give you a Shelleyan promise that the dialogue will come out complete.

CORSO: Beautiful. Because I tell you what you would be knocking out if you cut: the *spiritus*. You know what the *spiritus* is? It's the whole fire of this whole thing, you and I talking about all the subjects. Let it go. If you cut something, part of the *spiritus* is taken out. *Spiritus* is nothing to do with religion; it's the energy in a person and you're talking about very personal things and about this man's life. Right? If you were putting it on a particular segment for TV or the news it would be understandable that you'd want to count the ums and ahs, but you should have space to do the whole shot. If it's going to come out as words on a piece of paper then you show it to me. Then *I* know where the cutting comes. I am the word man that way.

SELERIE: You give me your address, I'll send you the transcript.

CORSO: What are you going to do with that pamphlet?

SELERIE: Put it out as part of a series. It's not a big commercial venture.

CORSO: Okay. Let's see how you type this out.

SELERIE: Do you want to stop?

CORSO: No, let's keep it going man. This is the ball game. Let's see what you got, how you type it out.

SELERIE: Because the punctuation and layout are going to be important.

CORSO: Yeah, yeah – very much so. You see, I didn't know that you were going to put this thing on to paper …

SELERIE: I thought I explained that the other night. You didn't think I was going to file it and forget about it? I didn't come over here just for personal research. You know that.

CORSO: Can I finish this? A man like me, when I put word to paper and I sign my name to it, I'm a poet man. I'm very careful about what I put on that paper.

SELERIE: I know you are.

CORSO: But if you take this tape here and transcribe it, people will read it on the page – they're gonna think I wrote that shit on the page. So you better make sure that they know, right off the bat, that I did not write this, that this is just a talk one night.

SELERIE: Okay, this is a second Shelleyan promise: that I will put in an introduction the circumstances of talking in Jay Landesman's house – these people coming round and the fact that it was a living event, not cold on the page.

CORSO: You know how it passes? If you just take it down the way you said it, the way I'm talking now – this is in it, right?

SELERIE: I'll keep the crooked and the straight – the whole journey.

CORSO: Then it works. You'll send me a copy though, before you spread it around.

SELERIE: Let's go back to Shelley. Shelley was grounded in the politics of his time; he knew what was happening on the street but he also had some larger spiritual awareness. There was no split like there is in some people. Do you feel you have a similar unity of outlook? So that you are talking about Nixon, Carter, all these people, at the same time that you're …

CORSO: I didn't mention Nixon and Carter, did I?

SELERIE: No, you mentioned the death of Kennedy and we talked about Hitler and Stalin.

CORSO: We did.

SELERIE: But is this quality which I see in Shelley your thing also?

CORSO: Where are my cigarettes, man?

(*End of tape*)

WHAT HAPPENED TO KEROUAC?
THE CORSO TRANSCRIPT
Lewis MacAdams

What Happened to Kerouac? *was conceived when Lewis MacAdams and I attended a weeklong conference in 1982 at Colorado's Naropa Institute, celebrating the 25th anniversary of the publication of Kerouac's seminal work,* On the Road. *We spent the week taping 21 hours of interviews with Kerouac's cronies and ex-lovers from the Beat movement. Everyone from Allen Ginsberg, Gregory Corso, and William Burroughs to Kerouac's daughter, Jan, and his first wife, Edie Kerouac Parker, contributed memories and anecdotes made remarkably vivid by the convergence at this event of the many people who knew Jack Kerouac.*

These interviews would become the backbone for the film. Yet for two years following the conference nothing happened with the footage. The project fell into limbo due to lack of money. It was wasteful and ridiculous to do nothing. I had filmed the Colorado interviews and knew how good the footage was. Then I raised some money and recruited my longtime friend Nick Dorsky, also a Kerouac fan and filmmaker, to edit the film.

In making the film we were trying to show some of these great people before they disappeared. We had a rule to only use people from the interviews that knew Kerouac personally. Gregory Corso became a main voice in the film, providing humor and a poet's insight. He had a lot to say, debunking a lot of the myths.

Richard Lerner

MacADAMS: Can you remember, like, some kind of time when you were talking to Kerouac where you guys, like, saw it, saw the way it was gonna come down?

CORSO: No way. I told you, I asked Ginsie [Ginsberg], "Did you know?" And he said "Yes." So I said, "You fucker, why didn't you tell me that? I would have bought all your early books." And they go for about 100 bucks apiece signed. Kerouac's *On the Road*, first edition signed, probably 500 bucks.[1] They could have told me.

MacADAMS: Yeah.

00:01:57

CORSO: I think they were bullshitting me, man. Are you kidding? They didn't know what was gonna happen. They *wanted* it to happen, but for themselves. It was individualistic.

MacADAMS: So the Beat Generation is after that ...

CORSO: America, America creates these individualists, right? But when they were all together – and it wasn't much – you don't call a generation four people, right? Four does not a generation make. That's why I think the weight fell on them. That's why Madison Avenue got on them, because they were the guys the same age as they, and they weren't *in* this generation. They were sort of, like, excluded, and they had the power game, they had the media and all that. That's why they downed Monsieur Kerouac.

00:12:14

MacADAMS: When you guys first met, like, where do you feel like you actually met? What was the meeting ground, you know?

CORSO: The meeting ground was that we were both good-looking guys.

MacADAMS: Uh huh.

CORSO: I had just come out of prison, and he just comes from the sea. From the sea, all right? And Ginsberg was praising him to me. And when he found out I wasn't a faggot and all that, then he went *double* towards me, 'cause most of Ginsberg's friends at the time were gay and all that shit. So, the rarity of a poet being non-faggot and having certain kinds of ideas that he had …

00:22:07

MacADAMS: So Allen can do it 'cause he can see it …

CORSO: Allen just knows what's happening. In the early Columbia days, he saw this beautiful Kerouac and he heard that he was a writer. Man, Allen went bananas. Dig it. And Burroughs has got the good head and all that, and he meets them there at Columbia and, bam, then you better believe they'll talk. They had no idea of a movement at the time and whatnot. Right? And I come at the tail end, the years of 1949, 1950.

00:25:40

CORSO: But a lot of people around that time were knowing. They just couldn't express it as well and whatnot. And the women, I mean, wow, they were so sharp. Now, girls had to go to the loony bin. Kerouac didn't go for it, or Ginsberg or me for what we said, but what *they* said, through action … went to the loony bin. Shock treatment and all that. This is 1949, 1950.

MacADAMS: You know, it's still happening in, like, 70 or 80 percent of the …

CORSO: Yeah, we know it's happening now but then, I'll tell you why the women weren't in the Beat Generation game. That's why Diane di Prima could slip through and say, "I'm one of them," but she's late. She's what? '56 or some shot. See what I'm saying?

MacADAMS: Yeah.

CORSO: So, like, the early … was the teachers … Hope … was a teacher of Kerouac and Ginsberg.

MacADAMS: Who was?

CORSO: This woman, Hope. Girl – she was 17. She knew *all* about the mantras. She knew all about Sengzhao[2] and Li Po.[3] They didn't know shit about it.

00:35:35

CORSO: He was a prose writer, all right, that had a lot of poetic things in it. He was not a poetry prose writer. What's it called? Prose poems?

MacADAMS: Yeah, yeah.

CORSO: No. No way. He was a prose writer.

MacADAMS: In the sense of meaning that he was a storyteller?

CORSO: But ... storyteller ... but the way he laid it down you would call poetic.

MacADAMS: So ...

CORSO: You got the idea?

MacADAMS: Yeah.

CORSO: Poetic. But if you'd ever seen poetic *writing* – prose – it's awful. It's so embarrassing. You got *Ushant* by Conrad Aiken. You got *The Enormous Room* by Cummings. I mean, yuck already. Forget it. Spare me.

MacADAMS: What was it that saved Kerouac? I mean, you think it was his, quote, genius? I mean ...

CORSO: What's this you're giving me about "saving"? What saved me? What saved him? Nobody, nothing saved him. He's out. He bit the dust. He was dusted, man.

MacADAMS: Yeah, but I mean something that made him, like, not write poetic prose, not write prose poems.

CORSO: He was a smart man. You mustn't forget this. He was a very intelligent baby. Very smart.

MacADAMS: You think the word "genius" applies?

CORSO: Oh yeah, yeah, yeah. "Genius" is easy for him, but "divine"? I don't know, and I think that's what this ... Kerouac, I think, is trying to lay down. 'Cause there are three stages: He's got talent, you're a genius, and then you hit the ball game – divine.

MacADAMS: I missed that last thought. "You hit the ball game ..."

CORSO: Divine.

MacADAMS: Divine.

CORSO: Yeah, yeah, yeah, yeah. There are three stages, all right? Now, talent. "Now that one had a good talent but too bad he blew it." Right? Didn't exercise his talent.

MacADAMS: Yeah.

CORSO: When they exercise their talent and it becomes really great they say "genius." Human beings give it the appellation "genius." But when it comes divine, watch out. It's the afterwards, and they're giving calls to Kerouac the divine shot.

MacADAMS: And you think that's ...

CORSO: Sure! Because of the influence. Who would you hit else that was divine in, let's say, lit ... we could do painting, we could do painting and music, but give me lit. Who's divine?

MacADAMS: Shelley.

CORSO: Yeah, you hit it. And that's the only one other.

MacADAMS: So what is the divine? What do you mean, "divine"?

CORSO: That's the third stage you gotta reach.

MacADAMS: Yeah, but what I mean, is it like "holy"? Is that what you mean by "divine"?

CORSO: No way! No way. No, no. It's *spiritus* – intellectual spirit all the way. Intellectual beauty all the way. That's what you talk about "saving." That's the thing. The makers and lovers of beauty save it.

00:40:40

CORSO: He knows the individual. That's America, man. America is digging the individual, being an individual. He dug Neal Cassady, the individual American, the prototype that *contained* Americana.

00:54:05

CORSO: He could take the appellation "poeta." A Bob Dylan, a Jim Morrison cannot, although on Morrison's grave is "Poet." Why do these rock and rollers who made all the bread and that want that top-class appellation? I know why.

MacADAMS: Why?

CORSO: It's pretty sad. You take the two things they knew, that the poet is with the kings and emperors. You see, it's right up there. Right? And they're just the minstrels.

MacADAMS: Haha.

CORSO: Take the ball game. Philosophy doesn't even hit with them. Okay. So they figure, uh oh, well, the lyrics became important to what you say and what they say, they make redundant; it's what's called "refrain." No wise king would want to hear somebody … hear repetitive in their ear.

01:05:46

MacADAMS: I was thinking about, like, were you around him at all when *On the Road* came out?

CORSO: Yeah. I was in San Francisco when he was just about to go off on the road. Ginsberg called him up and told him, "Gregory's there. Take him along." And he said, "No, I think I'll just go with Neal," so I couldn't have gone in with that.

MacADAMS: Do you regret not having gone in?

CORSO: No.

MacADAMS: But when the book itself was actually published, were you around him?

CORSO: Uh, yeah. Well, I was in Amsterdam and then we came back. We got a postcard from him, he telling us that *On the Road* was published and accepted.

MacADAMS: But did you start to see any change in him?

CORSO: Yeah, when I came back from Amsterdam he was drunk – first time I saw him drunk ...

MacADAMS: Oh, really?

CORSO: ... his face all reddened, and lolling in the adulation. And that was a knockout blow for him. I saw a different Kerouac.

MacADAMS: Already at that point ...

CORSO: Oh, sure.

01:14:36

CORSO: ... and what Kerouac did was something of beauty, and an influence. It opened up the head to beauty. When you open up the head to beauty, you open it up to spirit. Now, what is spirit? Most people have it ethereal; they have it, you know, up in the sky. Airy fairy bullshit. They do, the spirit. They don't know that spirit is a hard tough baby. You know? It really is. I mean, that's the one that outlasts the body. That's the one that hangs around the host, the body. Dig it. The classy spirit hangs around you. You shit, you fart and all that. The spirit's got to be there.

MacADAMS: Well, that's what I ... I feel like ...

CORSO: But the spirit's in the same thing. The spirit's gas, right? Any form you want to give it. You see, the spirit has no form, right? It *takes* you, right? And that's how you handle it.

01:21:45

MacADAMS: One of the things I always thought it seemed like, was that Jack was stuck at ... was, like, not knowing how to be an older man, like it seems like that his joy was about being a young man and he didn't know to deal with ...

CORSO: That's called crisis – middle age crisis game?

MacADAMS: Something. I don't know.

CORSO: I don't know. Everybody's got that shot, they say.

MacADAMS: Yeah, but it seemed like he was so ... he loved so much, like, the thing that he did when he was in his twenties that he didn't find anything that he could love as much, or something.

CORSO: I think it was, again, going after the "it," the success, and he got it and, on that basis, did not know how to handle it. And you gotta remember, the American media is a tough fucker, man. Really can get on you. They can say things on you that you never said and people get the image of you that way. Sure.

01:31:07

MacADAMS: Do you think that he'd felt he was written out? That he didn't have anything more to say?

CORSO: That, you mean, writer's block? I don't know.

MacADAMS: Not writer's block but just, like, "Hey, I already, you know like, I said it. Like, I said it."

CORSO: Yeah, that's the truth. He did say it. That's it. Then what do you do afterwards? So it's good now, if kids are watching this, to get another job. In other words, get a duad. If you want to be a writer, get another job and then work on your spare time on your writing. But if you want to be a poet, you can't be. You gotta know you *are* a poet, and then you got no fucking choice.

Oh, you got a choice. I'll tell you what. A poet ... a poet's fate is by choice. You choose it. You gotta know you're a poet. But you ain't gonna get the financial rewards. You're gonna get a lot of weight laid on you. They'll look at you as weird or something somehow, and I don't care if the style of your hair is long or short. Or you could get into the academy where it's stifled. Or you could see something new, and by seeing that something new that's here and nobody sees, and you illuminate others, then you got it made. So I'm happy being a poet 'cause I figure I saw something that no other people saw – at the same time as Ginsie, and Keroauc, and Burroughs – and laid it down. And that's why they call the Beat Generation a phenomenon. Right?

ENDNOTES

TWO POETS IN PARIS
pages 23–25

1. This transcription of "Bomb" differs from the version published by City Lights in 1958.

THE UPBEAT BEATNIK
pages 27–29

1. Henry Luce (1898–1967), American magazine publishing magnate.

2. The Sullivan Act was a gun control law enacted in New York State in 1911 which made the carrying of unlicensed concealed firearms a felony.

3. Dr. Norman Vincent Peale (1898–1993), American minister and author, most notably of *The Power of Positive Thinking* (1952).

SOME OF MY BEGINNING ... AND WHAT I FEEL RIGHT NOW
pages 33–41

1. Howard Nemerov, ed., *Poets on Poetry* (New York: Basic Books, 1966).

CONVERSATION WITH ALLEN GINSBERG & GREGORY CORSO
pages 43–45

1. The International Poetry Incantation at the Royal Albert Hall in London on June 11, 1965, drew an estimated crowd of 7,000. Readings were presented by Lawrence Ferlinghetti, Michael Horovitz, Gregory Corso, Harry Fainlight, Adrian Mitchell, Christopher Logue, Alexander Trocchi, Ernst Jandl, Pete Brown, Allen Ginsberg, John Esam, Spike Hawkins, Anselm Hollo, Paulo Leonni, George Macbeth, Tom McGrath, Daniel Richter, and Simon Vinkenoog. A recording of William Burroughs reading his work was also played in the hall. Andrei Voznesensky, Pablo Neruda, and Pablo Fernandez were in attendance but did not read. Peter Whitehead documented the event on film and released it as *Wholly Communion*.

2. Corso read "The Mutation of the Spirit: A Shuffle Poem," originally published in 1964 by Death Press and reprinted as "Mutation of the Spirit" in *Elegiac Feelings American* in 1970.

AN INTERVIEW WITH GREGORY CORSO
pages 47–87

1. *Dear Fathers* (Village Station, NY: Interim Books, 1972) was a collection of letters to a Benedictine monk calling for needed reforms in the Vatican.

2. "Ignu" is the title of a 1958 poem by Allen Ginsberg from his collection *Kaddish and Other Poems: 1958-1960* (City Lights, 1961). In an audio recording from the 1973 Kerouac Symposium held at Salem State College in Salem, Massachusetts, Ginsberg credited Jack Kerouac with coining the word in the late 1940s and defined the ignu as a "Gnostic ignoramus ... a great bullshit artist" and an "angel in comical form."

3. From the poem "Discord," *The Happy Birthday of Death* (1960).

4. From the poem "Hello," *Gasoline* (1958).

5. The Black Mountain poets, sometimes called projectivist poets, were a group of mid-20th century American avant-garde or postmodern poets centered in Black Mountain College in North Carolina.

6. From the poem "Mexican Impressions," *Gasoline* (1958).

7. Corso's 1961 novel, *American Express*, originally published by Olympia Press, has been available as a print-on-demand title from Disruptive Publishing since 2005.

8. John Cage (1912–1992), American avant-garde composer, writer, and artist.

9. "George Jackson" was written and recorded by Bob Dylan in November 1971 as a tribute to Black Panther leader, George Jackson, who had been shot and killed by guards at San Quentin Prison on August 21, 1971, an event that indirectly provoked the Attica Prison riot.

10. Carol Grilhiggen, a character in Corso's *American Express*.

11. The Cave of the Trois-Frères, located in southwestern France, is famous for its cave paintings which date from approximately 13,000 BC.

12. Richard Howard, "Gregory Corso," *Chelsea*, No. 22/23, 1968, pp. 148–57.

13. There is no Stowbridge in Massachusetts. Corso was likely referring to the town of Sturbridge, home of the Austen Riggs Center, a psychiatric treatment facility founded in 1913.

14. Joseph Conrad, *The Secret Agent* (1907).

15. "Says Poet Brodsky, Ex of the Soviet Union: 'A Writer Is a Lonely Traveler, and No One Is His Helper.'" *New York Times Magazine*, October 1, 1972.

16. James Laughlin (1914–1997), American poet and literary book publisher who founded New Directions Publishing in 1936.

17. The title of the poem that Corso was referring to is actually "Death of the American Indian's God."

18. "Spontaneous Requiem for the American Indian" from *Elegiac Feelings American* (1970).

HUMOR, THE BUTCHER: AN INTERVIEW WITH GREGORY CORSO
pages 89–92

1. Corso's poems from 1970 to 1974 were to be published in a book he planned to call *Who Am I – Who I Am*, but the manuscript was stolen and there were no other copies. In her article "The Enigmatic Relationship of Poets Isabella Gardner and Gregory Corso" (*The Journal of Beat Studies*, Volume 3, 2014: 111), writer Marian Janssen asserts that the stolen manuscript story was fabricated by Corso as "an excuse for his nonproductivity and a possibility to extort a considerable amount of money" from Gardner. (See also Gavin Selerie's interview with Corso, pages 156–157 of this book.)

2. In a 1971 letter to publisher James Laughlin, Corso wrote that "America Politica Historia" was originally published in 1960. Source: Bill Morgan, ed., *An Accidental Autobiography: The Selected Letters of Gregory Corso* (New York: New Directions, 2003), p. 403.

I'M POOR SIMPLE HUMAN BONES: AN INTERVIEW WITH GREGORY CORSO
pages 93–121

1. "The American Way" from *Elegiac Feelings American* (1970).

2. "Elegiac Feelings American (for the dear memory of John Kerouac)" from *Elegiac Feelings American* (1970).

3. "From the play *Summer's Last Will and Testament* (1592) by English playwright, poet and satirist Thomas Nashe (1567–1601).

4. A limited edition (309 copies) of "The Geometric Poem" was published by Litografia Cosmopresse, Milan, in 1966.

5. Beginning in October 1943, poet Robert Lowell served five months of a one-year sentence in federal prison for being a conscientious objector.

6. Kerouac's original manuscript of *On the Road*, the typewritten scroll, used the real names of the novel's protagonists. Prior to its 1957 publication by Viking Press, they were changed and, so, Allen Ginsberg became Carlo Marx.

7. Ettore Sottsass (1917–2007), Italian architect and designer, credited with bringing office equipment into the realm of popular culture with his design of the now classic bright red plastic Olivetti Valentine portable typewriter in 1969.

8. Bruce Cook, *The Beat Generation* (New York: Charles Scribner's Sons, 1971).

9. Lawrence Lipton's 1959 book, *Holy Barbarians*, was a sociological study of the West Coast Beat scene.

INTERVIEW: GREGORY CORSO
pages 123–131

1. The 16th arrondissement of Paris (also known as "Arrondissement de Passy") is one of the 20 administrative districts of Paris. Noted for its large avenues, prestigious schools, and high concentration of museums, it has long been known as one of French high society's favorite places of residence, comparable to New York's Upper East Side.

2. The book referred to, *Heirlooms from the Future*, was published in 1981 with the title *Herald of the Autochthonic Spirit*.

3. Sun Myung Moon (1920–2012), Korean religious leader, business magnate, and media mogul. A self-proclaimed messiah, Moon was the founder of the Unification Church.

4. Satchidananda Saraswati (1914–2002), Indian religious teacher, spiritual master, and yoga adept, who gained fame and following in the West during his time in New York City. He came to public attention as the opening speaker at the Woodstock music and arts festival in 1969.

5. Eldridge Cleaver (1935–1988), writer (*Soul on Ice*), political activist, and an early leader of the Black Panther Party. As a fugitive from the United States criminal justice system, he spent seven years in exile in Cuba, Algiers, and France, returning to the US in 1975.

6. Gordon Ball, ed., *Allen Verbatim: Lectures on Poetry, Politics, Consciousness* (New York: McGraw-Hill, 1974).

7. Martin Buber (1878–1965), Austrian-born Israeli Jewish philosopher best known for his philosophy of dialogue, a form of existentialism.

8. Les Halles, the central wholesale fresh food market of Paris since 1183, was demolished in 1971 and replaced with a modern underground shopping center.

POETRY POWER FOR A BLOODLESS COUP: AN INTERVIEW WITH GREGORY CORSO
pages 133–137

1. Corso was fired from the faculty of SUNY Buffalo on March 8, 1965, after refusing to sign the school's loyalty oath known as the "Feinberg Certificate," a document that all faculty and staff were required to sign certifying that they were not members of the Communist Party. Corso's action was part of a student-faculty protest against the dismissal of fellow Professor John Sporn for his false denial of past Communist Party membership. New York's Feinberg Law was adopted in 1949 and banned from the teaching profession anyone who belonged to a "subversive organization" or called for the overthrow of the government. The law, enacted during the height of the Red Scare, was specifically aimed at communists and remained in force until 1967 when a United States Supreme Court decision declared most of its provisions unconstitutional.

2. According to his obituary in the *San Francisco Examiner* (January 13, 1986), poet Bob Kaufman (1926–1986) inspired journalist Herb Caen to coin the phrase "beatnik" after he, "in a fit of poetic and/or alcoholic ecstasy, kicked the window out of the Co-Existence Bagel Shop while commenting on current events: 'Sputnik! Sputnik!'"

THE RIVERSIDE INTERVIEWS: 3 GREGORY CORSO
pages 139–175

1. The original publication of *The Riverside Interviews: 3* also included essays on Corso by Jim Burns and Michael Horovitz.

2. The first Poetry Olympics was held on September 26, 1980, and, in addition to Corso, featured poets John Cooper Clarke, Michael Horovitz, Frances Horovitz, Janine Pommy Vega, and Linton Kwesi Johnson.

3. *Dont Look Back* was D.A. Pennebaker's 1967 film documenting Bob Dylan's 1965 concert tour in the United Kingdom. There is no apostrophe in the film's title.

4. Isabella "Belle" Gardner (1915–1981), poet, actress, and an associate editor of *Poetry* magazine from 1952 to 1956. She was the cousin of poet Robert Lowell and great-niece of art collector Isabella Stewart Gardner.

5. Thomas Berger (1924–2014), American novelist.

WHAT HAPPENED TO KEROUAC? THE CORSO TRANSCRIPT
pages 177–185

1. The going price in 2014 for a first edition copy of *On the Road* signed by Kerouac was between $20,000 and $28,000 USD.

2. Sengzhao (384–414 AD), Chinese Buddhist philosopher.

3. Li Po (701–762 AD), Chinese poet, also known as Li Bai.

LITERARY FIGURES MENTIONED IN THE INTERVIEWS

Aiken, Conrad (1889–1973), American novelist and poet. Recipient of the Pulitzer Prize in 1930 for his *Selected Poems*.

Alighieri, Dante (1265–1321), major Italian poet of the Middle Ages and author of the *Divine Comedy*.

Ashbery, John (born 1927), American poet. Recipient of the Pulitzaer Prize in 1976 for his collection *Self-Portrait in a Convex Mirror*.

Auden, W.H. (1907–1973), Anglo-American poet, born in England and later an American citizen. Recipient of the Pulitzer Prize in 1948 for *The Age of Anxiety*.

Baraka, Amiri (born LeRoi Jones; 1934–2014), American poet, playwright, novelist, essayist, and music critic. Founded Totem Press and the poetry magazine *Yugen* (1958–1962) which published works by such writers as Jack Kerouac, Allen Ginsberg, Gregory Corso, Frank O'Hara, Gary Snyder, Michael McClure, and Philip Whalen.

Baudelaire, Charles Pierre (1821–1867), French poet, essayist, art critic, and translator of Edgar Allan Poe, best known for *Les Fleurs du Mal*.

Bellow, Saul (1915–2005), Canadian-born American writer and winner of the Pulitzer Prize, the Nobel Prize in Literature (1976), and the National Medal of Arts. Works include *The Adventures of Augie March* (1953), *Seize the Day* (1956), *Henderson the Rain King* (1959), *Herzog* (1964), and *Humboldt's Gift* (1976).

Benedikt, Michael (1935–2007), American poet, editor, and literary critic.

Berger, John (born 1926), English art critic, novelist, painter, and poet whose novel *G.* won the 1972 Booker Prize.

Berryman, John (1914–1972), American poet and scholar and a key figure in the Confessional school of poetry.

Breton, André (1896–1966), French writer, poet, and founder of Surrealism.

Brodsky, Joseph (1940–1996), Russian poet and essayist, expelled from the Soviet Union in 1972. Awarded the 1987 Nobel Prize in Literature and appointed United States Poet Laureate in 1991.

Browning, Robert (1812–1889), Victorian English poet and playwright.

Brukenfeld, Richard (born 1933), American playwright and publisher of Corso's first volume of poems, *The Vestal Lady on Brattle* (1955).

Burroughs, William S. (1914–1997), American novelist, short story writer, essayist, painter, spoken word performer, and primary figure of the Beat Generation. Works include *Junkie*

(1953), *Naked Lunch* (1959), and *The Nova Trilogy* (1961–67).

Byron, (Lord) George Gordon (1788–1824), English poet and a leading figure in the Romantic Movement.

Carlyle, Thomas (1795–1881), Scottish philosopher, satirical writer, essayist, historian, and teacher.

Carr, Lucien (1925–2005), key member of the original New York City circle of the Beat Generation in the 1940s and, later, editor for United Press International.

Carruth, Hayden (1921–2008), American poet and literary critic.

Cassady, Neal (1926–1968), major figure of the Beat Generation in the 1950s and the psychedelic and counterculture movements of the 1960s. Author of *The First Third* (1971).

Céline, Louis-Ferdinand (1894–1961), French novelist, pamphleteer, and physician.

Clarke, Henderson (1887–1958), American writer and journalist known for his romantic novels, mystery fiction, and screenplays.

Clarke, John Cooper (born 1949), English performance poet who first became famous during the punk rock era of the late 1970s when he became known as a "punk poet." Author of *Ten Years In an Open-Necked Shirt and other Poems* (1981).

Conrad, Joseph (1857–1924), Polish author who wrote in English after settling in England. Works include *Lord Jim* (1900), *The Secret Agent* (1907), and *The Secret Sharer* (1910).

Crane, Hart (1899–1932), modernist American poet. Author of *White Buildings* (1926) and the long poem *The Bridge* (1930).

Creeley, Robert (1926–2005), American poet and author associated with the Black Mountain poets.

Chrétien de Troyes (?), late 12th-century French poet and known for his work on Arthurian subjects, and for originating the character Lancelot.

Cummings, E.E. (1894–1962), American poet, painter, essayist, author, and playwright.

di Prima, Diane (born 1934), American poet and participant in the emerging Beat Movement of the 1950s and 1960s.

Dickenson, Emily (1830–1886), reclusive American poet.

Duncan, Robert (1919–1988), American poet and follower of Western esotericism. Often identified with Black Mountain College and also a key figure in the San Francisco Renaissance.

Dunsany, Lord (Edward Plunkett; 1878–1957), Irish writer and dramatist and 18th Baron of Dunsany, most noted for his fantasy short stories.

Eliot, T.S. (1888–1965), essayist, publisher, playwright, literary, social critic, and one of the 20th century's major poets. Notable works include *The Love Song of J. Alfred Prufrock* (1915) and *The Waste Land* (1922).

Ferlinghetti, Lawrence (born 1919), American poet, painter, liberal activist, and co-founder of City Lights Booksellers & Publishers. Author of *A Coney Island of the Mind* (1958).

Fernandez, Pablo (born 1930), Cuban poet, novelist, essayist, and playwright. 1996 recipient of the National Prize for Literature, Cuba's most prestigious literary award.

Ginsberg, Allen (1926–1997), American poet and one of the leading figures of both the Beat Generation of the 1950s and the counterculture that soon would follow. Works include *Howl* *and Other Poems* (1956), *Kaddish and Other Poems* (1961), *Reality Sandwiches* (1963), and *Mind Breaths* (1978).

Giorno, John (born 1936), American poet and performance artist. Founder of the not-for-profit production company Giorno Poetry Systems and organizer of a number of early multimedia poetry experiments and events, including Dial-A-Poem.

Hölderlin, Friedrich (1770–1843), major German lyric poet, commonly associated with the artistic movement known as Romanticism.

Holmes, John Clellon (1926–1988), American author, poet, and professor, best known for his 1952 novel *Go*, considered the first "Beat" novel.

Horovitz, Frances (1938–1983), English poet and BBC broadcaster.

Horovitz, Michael (born 1935), English poet, artist, translator, and founder of the *New Departures* publications in 1959.

Howard, Richard (born 1929), American poet, literary critic, essayist, teacher, and translator. Longtime poetry editor of *The Paris Review*. Recipient of the National Book Award for his 1983 translation of Baudelaire's *Les Fleurs du Mal*.

Hugo, Victor (1802–1885), French poet, novelist, and dramatist of the Romantic Movement. Author of *Les Misérables* and *Notre-Dame de Paris* (*The Hunchback of Notre Dame*).

Hunt, Leigh (1784–1859), English critic, essayist, poet, and writer.

Jarrell, Randall (1914–1965), American poet, literary critic, children's author, essayist, novelist, and the 11th Consultant in Poetry to the Library of Congress, a position that now bears the title Poet Laureate.

Jong, Erica (born 1942), American author and teacher best known for her fiction and poetry, and particularly for her 1973 novel *Fear of Flying*.

Jonson, Ben (1572–1637), English playwright, poet, and literary critic.

Joyce, James (1882–1941), Irish novelist and poet, considered to be one of the most influential writers in the modernist avant-garde of the early 20th century. Major works include *Dubliners* (1914), *A Portrait of the Artist as a Young Man* (1916), *Ulysses* (1922), and *Finnegans Wake* (1939).

Kaufman, Bob (1925–1986), American Beat poet and surrealist inspired by jazz music. In France, where his poetry had a large following, he was known as the "black American Rimbaud."

Keats, John (1795–1821), English Romantic poet.

Koch, Kenneth (1925–2002), American poet, playwright, and professor. He was a prominent poet of the New York School of poetry, a loose group of poets including Frank O'Hara and John Ashbery.

Kerouac, Jack (1922–1969), American novelist, poet, and pioneer of the Beat Movement. Works include *The Town and the City* (1950), *On the Road* (1957), *The Subterraneans* (1958), *The Dharma Bums* (1958), *Mexico City Blues* (1959), and *Visions of Cody* (1960).

Lamantia, Philip (1927–2005), American poet and lecturer. His work was anthologized in *Penguin Modern Poets, No. 13* alongside that of Charles Bukowski and Harold Norse. One of the five poets (including Allen Ginsberg, Michael McClure, Gary Snyder, and Philip Whalen) who read at the famous San Francisco Six Gallery reading in 1955.

Laughlin, James (1914–1997), American poet and literary book publisher who founded New Directions Publishing in 1936.

Lawrence, D.H. (1885–1930), English novelist, poet, playwright, essayist, literary critic, and painter. Novels include *Sons and Lovers* (1913), *The Rainbow* (1915), *Women in Love* (1920), and *Lady Chatterley's Lover* (1928).

Lipton, Lawrence (1898–1975), American journalist, writer, and poet. Author of *The Holy Barbarians* (1959).

Lowell, Robert (1917–1977), American poet whose poems were frequently set in Boston and the New England region. Winner of the 1960 National Book Award for *Life Studies*.

MacLeish, Archibald (1892–1982), American poet, writer, and the Librarian of Congress. Associated with the Modernist school of poetry. Recipient of three Pulitzer Prizes (1933, 1953, and 1959), a Tony Award for Best Drama (1959), an Academy Award for Documentary Feature (1965), and the Presidential Medal of Freedom (1977).

Mailer, Norman (1923–2007), American novelist, journalist, essayist, playwright, filmmaker, and actor. Works include *The Naked and the Dead* (1948) and *The Executioner's Song* (1979).

Marlowe, Christopher (1564–1593), English dramatist, poet, and translator of the Elizabethan era.

McClure, Michael (born 1932), American poet, playwright, songwriter, and novelist. One of the five poets (including Allen Ginsberg, Philip Lamantia, Gary Snyder, and Philip Whalen) who read at the famous San Francisco Six Gallery reading in 1955. The character of Pat McLear in Kerouac's *Big Sur* (1962) is based on McClure.

Michaux, Henri (1899–1984), Belgian-born poet, writer, and painter who wrote in French. Notable works include *My Properties* (1929), *Plume* (1938), and *Miserable Miracle* (1956).

Moore, Marianne (1887–1972), American Modernist poet and 1952 National Book Award winner for her *Collected Poems*.

Murao, Shigeyoshi "Shig" (1926–1999), American poet noted for being the City Lights clerk arrested in 1957 for selling Allen Ginsberg's *Howl* to an undercover San Francisco police officer.

Neruda, Pablo (1904–1973), Chilean poet-diplomat and politician. Recipient of the Nobel Prize for Literature in 1971.

Nochlin, Linda (born 1931), American art historian, university professor, and writer. Noted for her essay "Why Have There Been No Great Women Artists?" which appeared in *ARTnews* in 1971.

O'Brien, Flann (1911–1966), pen name of Irish novelist, playwright, and satirist Brian O'Nolan, considered a major figure in 20th century Irish and postmodern literature. Notable works include *At Swim-Two-Birds* (1939) and *The Third Policeman* (written between 1939 and 1940 and published posthumously in 1967).

O'Hara, Frank (1926–1966), American writer, poet, art critic, curator at the Museum of Modern Art, and a prominent figure in New York City's art world. His collections of poetry include *Meditations in an Emergency* (1957) and *Lunch Poems* (1964).

Olson, Charles (1910–1970), American modernist poet associated with the Black Mountain School. A proponent of projective verse which favored a poetic meter based on sound and the poet's breathing rather than syntax and logic.

Orlovsky, Peter (1933–2010), American poet, actor, and longtime partner of Allen Ginsberg. His best-known collection of poetry was *Clean Asshole Poems & Smiling Vegetable Songs* (1978).

Plath, Sylvia (1932–1963), American poet, novelist, and short story writer. Works include *The Colossus and Other Poems* (1960), *The Bell Jar* (1963), and *Ariel* (1965). Her *Collected Poems* won the Pulitzer Prize for Poetry in 1982.

Poe, Edgar Allen (1809–1849), American author, poet, editor, and literary critic, considered part of the American Romantic Movement.

Pope, Alexander (1688–1744), English poet, best known for his satirical verse.

Pound, Ezra (1885–1972), expatriate American poet and critic and major figure of the early modernist movement. Best-known works include *Ripostes* (1912), *Hugh Selwyn Mauberley* (1920), and the unfinished 120-section epic, *The Cantos* (1917–69).

Pynchon, Thomas (born 1937), American novelist and short story writer. Best known for his early novels *V.* (1963), *The Crying of Lot 49* (1966), and *Gravity's Rainbow* (1973).

Ransom, John Crowe (1888–1974), educator, scholar, literary critic, poet, essayist and editor. First editor of *The Kenyon Review* literary journal.

Rexroth, Kenneth (1905–1982), American poet, translator, critical essayist, and a central figure in the San Francisco Renaissance. Dubbed the "Father of the Beats" by *Time* although he did not consider himself to be a Beat poet and disliked the association. Among the first poets in the United States to explore traditional Japanese poetic forms such as haiku.

Rhys, Jean (1890–1979), Dominican-born novelist, best known for her novel *Wide Sargasso Sea* (1966).

Rimbaud, Arthur (1854–1891), French poet who, as part of the decadent movement, influenced modern literature and arts, and prefigured surrealism.

Rothenberg, Jerome (born 1931), American poet, translator, and anthologist, noted for his work in the fields of ethnopoetics and performance poetry.

Schwerner, Armand (1927–1999), Belgian-born avant-garde American poet.

Shelley, Mary (born Mary Wollstonecraft Godwin; 1797–1851), English novelist, short story writer, dramatist, essayist, biographer, and travel writer, best known for her Gothic novel *Frankenstein: or, The Modern Prometheus* (1818).

Shelley, Percy Bysshe (1792–1822), English Romantic poet regarded by critics as one of the finest lyric poets in the English language. Major works include *The Necessity of Atheism* (1811) and *Prometheus Unbound* (1820).

Snyder, Gary (born 1930), American poet, essayist, lecturer, and environmental activist often associated with the Beat Generation and the San Francisco Renaissance. Winner of the Pulitzer Prize for Poetry for *Turtle Island* in 1975. One of the five poets (including Allen Ginsberg, Philip Lamantia, Michael McClure, and Philip Whalen) who read at the famous San Francisco Six Gallery reading in 1955.

Stendhal (1783–1842), pen name of Marie-Henri Beyle. 19th-century French writer. Known for such novels as *Le Rouge et le Noir* (*The Red and the Black*, 1830) and *La Chartreuse de Parme* (*The Charterhouse of Parma*, 1839).

Swinburne, Algernon Charles (1837–1909), English poet, playwright, novelist, and critic. Nominated for the Nobel Prize in Literature in every year from 1903 to 1907 and again in 1909.

Tarn, Nathaniel (born 1928), Parisian-born American poet, essayist, anthropologist, and translator.

Tate, Allen (1899–1979), American poet, essayist, social commentator, and Poet Laureate Consultant in Poetry to the Library of Congress from 1943 to 1944.

Thomas, Dylan (1914–1953), Welsh poet and writer known for such works as *Portrait of the Artist as a Young Dog* (1940), *A Child's Christmas in Wales* (1952), and *Under Milk Wood* (1954).

Van Doren, Mark (1894–1972), American poet, writer, critic, and professor of English at Columbia University for nearly 40 years. Literary editor of *The Nation* (1924–1928). Recipient of the 1940 Pulitzer Prize for Poetry for *Collected Poems 1922–1938*.

Villon, François (1431–1463), French poet, thief, and vagabond of the late Middle Ages. Best known for *Le Testament* (1461), written while in prison, which includes the poem "Ballade des dames du temps jadis" ("Ballad of the Ladies of Times Past").

Voznesensky, Andrei (1933–2010), Soviet and Russian poet and writer who Robert Lowell referred to as "one of the greatest living poets in any language." Best known for his unusual rhymes, he was often criticized by orthodox Soviet writers.

Whalen, Philip (1923–2002), American poet, Zen Buddhist, and a key figure in the San Francisco Renaissance. One of the five poets (including Allen Ginsberg, Philip Lamantia, Michael McClure, and Gary Snyder) who read at the famous San Francisco Six Gallery reading in 1955.

Whitman, Walt (1819–1892), American poet, essayist, and journalist. Often called the father of free verse, his work was controversial in its time, particularly his poetry collection *Leaves of Grass* (1855), which was described as obscene for its overt sexuality.

Williams, William Carlos (1883–1963), American poet closely associated with modernism and imagism. Major works include *Kora in Hell* (1920), *Spring and All* (1923), and *Pictures from Brueghel and Other Poems* (1962).

Woolf, Virginia (1882–1941), English writer and one of the foremost modernists of the 20th century. Most famous works include the novels *Mrs Dalloway* (1925), *To the Lighthouse* (1927), and *Orlando* (1928), and the book-length essay *A Room of One's Own* (1929).

Wordsworth, William (1770–1850), English poet who, with Samuel Taylor Coleridge, helped launch the Romantic Age in English literature with the joint publication of *Lyrical Ballads, with a Few Other Poems* (1798).

Yeats, William Butler (1865–1939), Irish poet and 1923 recipient of the Nobel Prize in Literature.

Yevtushenko, Yevgeny (born 1932), Soviet and Russian poet, novelist, essayist, dramatist, screenwriter, actor, editor, and film director. Described in 1991 by the *The Washington Times* as "his country's most controversial modern poet, a man whose reputation is poised between courageous behind-the-scenes reformer and failed dissident."

ACKNOWLEDGEMENTS

I would like to acknowledge everyone who had a part in making this book a reality. In addition to those who graciously allowed me to reprint their work in this volume, there were several individuals who generously contributed their time and effort by tracking down copies of old literary magazines, sending me scans and photographs, helping me get in contact with copyright holders, and so on. My sincere thanks go to Chrystal Alberts, Michael Annis, Costanzo Allione, Michael Andre, Juliet Ash, James Birmingham of RealityStudio.org, Victor Bockris, Dick Brukenfeld, Jennifer Buchwald, Tamara Buchwald, Ian Clifford, Jane Dalrymple-Hollo, Don DeMaio, Elsa Dorfman, Tony Frazer, Josh Gosciak, Peter Hale of The Allen Ginsberg Project, Marian Janssen, Foxy Kidd, Robert King, Arthur and Kit Knight, Richard Lerner, Lewis MacAdams, Kaye McDonough, James McKenzie, Fred Misurella, Kristina Moore, William Norris, Hank O'Neal, Tom Plante, Liza Richardson, Gavin Selerie, and Suzette Martinez Standring. Thanks also to the Allen Ginsberg Estate and Morden Tower, Newcastle upon Tyne, England.

I would also like to recognize the staff at the following libraries for their valuable assistance: the Morton R. Godine Library at the Massachusetts College of Art and Design, Trexler Library at Muhlenberg College, Special Collections at St. Lawrence University, Salem State University Library, Green Library at Stanford University, the Frank Melville, Jr. Memorial Library at Stony Brook University, the Special Collections Research Center at Syracuse University, the Louis Round Wilson Special Collections Library at the University of North Carolina at Chapel Hill, and the Rare Book and Manuscript Library at the University of Pennsylvania.

Thanks also to the following, without whose generous support this book may never have seen the light of day: JC Bauer, Maria Pargoli Bishop, Geoff and Wendy Blake, Regina Boratgis, The Magnificent Magdalen Bresee, Dan Buckle, Roger Bygott, Dave and Joan Carr, Clara Casian, painter

Jonathan Collins, Rob Cooper, Evan Cordes, Charles Cotter, Martha Cox, Walter F. Croft (his own self), Rick Dale, Cat de Leon, Pamela de Oliveira-Smith, David Depestel, Denise Enck of Empty Mirror Books, John Feins, Bruce Frederick, Marlys Backman Furze, Bob Geary, Martin Georgi, Deb Gowen, Mark Greeley, Sonia Weinstock Hamel, Alina Haverty, Kaarina Hollo, Tamsin Hollo, Chris Jones, R. L. "Bob" Jones, John Kelly of Toronto, Justine K. and Ronald King, Mat Kondo, Don and Trish La Rocca, Mary Jo Larson, Buck and Nadine Lombard, Blandine Longre-Stubbs of Black Herald Press, The Luddecke Family, Clark County (WA) Poet Laureate Christopher Luna, Mandolin and Tom-Tom, Richard Marsh, Peter McGee, Atticus McKennon-Peterson, Heidi Metzger, Judy Mintz, Thurston Moore, William Nesbitt, Timothy A. Nolan, David North-Martino, Danny Paige, Bob Plourde, Poems-For-All, Andrija Popovic, Mich Rygiel, Ismael Santos, Christopher H. Sartisohn, Ben Schafer, Juergen Schmidt, The Schober-Marquis Family, George Scrivani, Tricia Sicard, Austin J. Simpson, T. Kilgore Splake, Gia Stark, Rich Sullivan, Jeff Suwak, Tate Swindell, Lora Templeton, Anthony Vitale, Scarlett Watters, and Robert Whiteley (a.k.a. The Poet's Pulpit).

Finally, a special thanks to Michael Skau, Professor Emeritus at the University of Nebraska at Omaha and author of *A Clown in a Grave: Complexities and Tensions in the Works of Gregory Corso*, for sharing a couple of obscure pieces from his personal collection and clarifying some of the more ambiguous references in the interviews.

INDEX

CPSIA information can be obtained
at www.ICGtesting.com
Printed in the USA
FSHW020810051120
75480FS